Discover Atlantis

Discover Atlantis

A Guide to Reclaiming the Wisdom of the Ancients

DIANA COOPER AND SHAARON HUTTON

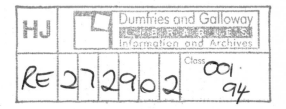

**HODDER
MOBIUS**

First published in Great Britain in 2005 by Hodder and Stoughton
A division of Hodder Headline

A Mobius Book

1

A CIP catalogue record for this title is available from the British Library

ISBN 0 340 83851 5

Typeset in ITC Berkeley by
Phoenix Typesetting, Auldgirth, Dumfriesshire

Printed and bound in Great Britain by
Mackays of Chatham Ltd, Chatham, Kent

Hodder Headline's policy is to use papers that are natural, renewable
and recyclable products and made from wood grown in sustainable
forests. The logging and manufacturing processes are expected to
conform to the environmental regulations of the country of origin.

Hodder and Stoughton Ltd
A division of Hodder Headline
338 Euston Road
London NW1 3BH

To the memory of Peter Hutton, my Dad,
who died during the writing of this book.

Diana dedicates this book to her beautiful
grand-daughter, Isabel, who is bringing in
the higher energy for the future.

Acknowledgements

We would like to thank Linda Powell for her support and help and Marion Battes for the information she so kindly shared; also Katrina Raphaell for her incredible books on crystals.

Illustrations for the dream catcher and the labyrinth from www.geocities.com and www.lessons4living.com respectively.

Contents

The Aim of the Book

In Golden Atlantis, for 1,500 years, the spiritual energy on our planet was the highest it has ever been. It was a time of heaven on Earth when everyone had incredible spiritual power. Now we have the opportunity to bring the energy of pure Atlantis back. Diana Cooper and Shaaron Hutton were asked by their guide, Kumeka, to explain the extraordinary gifts, qualities and powers that existed in the Golden Age. We were also asked to include in this book special exercises that will allow you to develop these skills for yourselves.

About the Authors

Diana's Story

Shaaron and I spent the evening of 31 December 1994 together, intending to meditate and write our New Year's resolutions. When we meditated together, the most extraordinary occurrence took place. A huge energy entered the room and both of us were given the same message. We were told that this presence was Kumeka, Lord of Light. He came from a different universe and explained that Earth had now earned the right to have his guidance. He was the Master of the Eighth Ray, which was due to enter this planet bringing clarity and deep transmutation. He said that he had watched us both for many years and had brought us together to work with him. I had been living in the West Indies when he first noticed my energy and for the next fifteen years he acted to ensure we met.

The energy of Kumeka was so overpowering that I still remember it as one of the most exciting and life-changing events of my entire life. At first we both had to be together to connect with him. Since then Shaaron has become incredibly psychic and clairvoyant. She can see Kumeka and has a direct communication with him, receiving very specific information and answers to questions. I work differently and he downloads chunks of spiritual knowledge to me, often when I am sitting at the computer or am out walking. He also makes sure I read or come across any other information I need. Occasionally he writes information across my third eye.

Now, for the first time, he has asked us to write this book on

Atlantis together so that people can help to bring back the energy of pure Atlantis. This has been a fascinating and awe-inspiring project and our thanks, love and gratitude go to Kumeka and the angels.

AN ANGEL VISITATION

With the guidance of my angels and spiritual masters I have written thirteen books and produced many CDs, crystal CD packs, angel cards and oracles. I spend much of my time travelling round the world with the intention of inspiring people with higher spiritual understandings. But it was not always so. Just over twenty years ago I was in the depth of despair over my impending divorce. I had no psychic, religious or spiritual background and more important I had no self-worth or confidence. I could see no future ahead. One day I cried out in anguish for help and an angel appeared. It was a golden being of light, about six feet tall. This wonderful being took me on a journey and showed me my future. When I returned I understood cosmic concepts that I had never previously considered. Slowly my life mission started.

At that time my greatest desire was to be a healer and to help people. I trained to be a hypnotherapist, counsellor and healer, and soon learnt that this is a fast track to personal and spiritual growth, for every client I saw was a mirror of something within me. If three clients presented with the same problem, I would look very hard at myself and gradually I became wiser.

For years I worked with my guides and was occasionally aware of angels around. With guidance I wrote my first four spiritual books and then, suddenly and dramatically, my life changed again. While I was lying in the bath, an angelic voice told me that they wanted me to introduce people to angels. I argued that I did not know anything about angels and did not want to do that. I really thought the world would think I was crazy. Eventually, I agreed and three angels appeared in front of me and gave me much information, which later became my first angel book, *A Little Light on Angels*. From that time I have worked closely with the angels and then with the archangels, masters and eventually Kumeka, my guide and master.

However, the angels are sometimes hard task masters. Because they have never experienced a physical body they do not understand physical limitations. I was working really hard to finish my first spiritual novel, *The Silent Stones*, before I left for a six-month trip to Australia. The angels woke me up in the middle of the night and surrounded my bed. I felt as if I was levitating and was filled with a sense of awe and love. The angels told me I was to write a book called *Angel Inspiration* and they wanted me to start immediately. Then they cocooned me back to sleep. In the morning I knew I had no alternative but to set aside *The Silent Stones* and start on *Angel Inspiration*. I could feel the angels enfolding me as I sat at the computer writing for fourteen hours a day, until it was finished. Then I just had time to complete the novel before I set off on my travels.

In Australia, I talked to many Aborigine elders and learnt about their sacred wisdom and connections with Lemuria. I wove their ancient wisdom, with esoteric secrets of Atlantis and Lemuria, into a second novel, *The Codes of Power*. Then, most exciting of all, I was introduced to the angels of Atlantis, who are returning with a message for us now. This became the start of the third novel, *The Web of Light*, which was set in Africa and was fascinating to conceive and write.

Now our guide, Kumeka, Master of the Eighth Ray, has expanded on the information revealed in the novels, as it is becoming more urgent to reclaim the energy of Atlantis. You will find more information than this book will allow about the twelve rays, the Illumined Ones and the new spiritual hierarchy, as well as the colours and purposes of the higher chakras, in my book *A New Light on Ascension* (see Further Reading).

For twenty years I have been on my own journey of personal

development and spiritual growth, travelling to all the places described in my books and many others. At the same time, I have been privileged to share my experiences and understandings in talks and workshops around the world. And now I offer you this book that Shaaron and I have written together. It has been a fascinating project and writing it has changed my life. I believe it can change your life too – and the world.

Shaaron's story

I was born 'knowing'. Even as a small child I was the person that my friends came to for guidance and support. My creative energy was utilised by making up stories and writing plays, which I directed and starred in. Like so many people, when I left school and went into the adult world this energy dissolved into the rigors of survival.

In my adult years, I developed migraines until they made life unbearable. My doctor sent me to Diana, who was at that time a hypnotherapist. We soon realised that the headaches were a manifestation of the blocking of my third eye and, as we worked together using hypnosis, my clairvoyant abilities became stronger, clearer and more sharply honed while the original symptoms disappeared. We also realised much later that this was how our spirit guide, Kumeka, brought us together so that we could connect directly with him.

Kumeka has come from another universe and is here now to help Earth and all of us on our journey to ascension. His energy is anchoring more and more powerfully into the planet as his ray, the Eighth Ray of Transmutation, enters Earth. My experience with Kumeka is grounded and fun. I consider him a beloved friend and have a very special relationship with him, which I value and enjoy. Although Kumeka has never incarnated on Earth, and so has never had a human body, my projection of him is a very tall broad bearded and strong man who exudes a very beautiful, gentle and often playful energy. At first Diana and I had to be together to connect with him, but very quickly I could sense what he was imparting and I could see him clearly. Now he is as visible as a physical human being. When I am taking a decision I can literally feel a hand on my shoulder, holding me back or encouraging me forward as appropriate. When we were working on this book, if I was unable to grasp a concept he would write or draw the information on a blackboard in my third eye.

Originally he communicated only with Diana and me, but now he can work through millions of people at a time. In order that people could get to know about him and connect with his energy, he asked me to commission someone to write music that would express all of his qualities, from his strength and incisiveness to his power and glory. Diana and I asked Andrew Brel to compose what is now the *Music for Kumeka* CD. Later Kumeka said that it was important for a new wave of light to go out across the planet. In order for this to happen he requested that we put together a set of crystal meditation CD packs. Under his direction we produced a set of six, using crystals, colour, music and a guided meditation to enable people to make higher connections with angels and archangels.

From palmistry and other psychic sources I have always understood that I would not find my true spiritual path until I reached my fifties, and so this has proved to be. The first thing Kumeka initiated was my doing soul readings to help other people understand their pathway in this lifetime. Now he has guided Diana and me to work together on this important book. I hope you gain as much value from reading it as we have from writing it.

CHAPTER 1

The Establishment
of Atlantis

Atlantis was a landmass between Europe and America, which is now submerged beneath the Atlantic Ocean. For 240,000 years this continent was the subject of a divine experiment to see if people could live in a physical body and still keep their connection with All That Is (known as the Creator, God, Godhead or Source). Throughout this long period, tests were set up in a number of different ways, but each time they were terminated as it became clear that humans with free will moved deeper into matter and self-destruction and further from their Source. When the conditions were reset for the fifth and last time, Golden Atlantis emerged. For a period of 1,500 years, the people maintained their purity and oneness with their Creator, and enjoyed awesome spiritual, psychic and technological powers. This book explains how they lived, their practices and what we can do today to return to that state.

Originally, the Source sent out aspects of itself, known as divine sparks or Monads, into all dimensions of the universes to experience and grow. The intention was that they would ultimately bring their experiences back to the Godhead. Some were to come to Earth, where they would have freedom to make their own decisions. Such a vast undertaking needed to be managed and the Intergalactic Council, made up of cosmic energies, was formed to oversee the operation.

Earth was always a special place, for it was pivotal in balancing the energy of our universe because of its connection to the Great Central Sun. Here, several exciting ventures took place, first in Mu, a continent in the South Atlantic, though none of these inhabitants incarnated in Atlantis. A later venture took place in Lemuria, a continent in the Southern Hemisphere, where the Lemurians were created. They were ethereal, without physical form as we understand it, and were androgynous, therefore complete in themselves, reproducing by conscious will and energy transference. However, their state of self-containment meant they had few challenges through which to grow.

At first they remained totally psychic and telepathic, maintaining their pure energy and oneness with Source. But, as time passed, their essence became discontented. They could perceive, as all spirits can, but they wanted to experience senses. They had never made love or touched a blade of grass. Nor had they tasted food, smelt the sweetness of a rose or felt the soft texture of a loved one's cheek. They longed to know what it is like to go deeper into matter with a physical body; to enjoy sexuality, touch, taste, smell, sight and hearing. They petitioned Source for this.

The Source of All That Is knew that if this was acceded to, the physical beings could become self-indulgent and hedonistic; that the allurement of the senses might tempt them away from their spiritual wisdom into the illusions of the flesh. So a deal was offered. They were told that their request would be granted on certain conditions. They could incarnate to partake of all the senses as long as they agreed to feel the related emotions. It was believed that because emotions are grounding, this would make people take responsibility for their actions, which in turn would become a catalyst for spiritual seeking and understanding.

With the granting of their request, each soul divided into two beings: one masculine and one feminine. In order to reproduce they now had to copulate with another human of the opposite sex. At last they had the opportunity to see, touch, hear, taste and smell – and to feel emotions. For these beings in bodies of flesh, the continent of Atlantis was prepared, which at first linked Africa, Europe, North America and South America. Those brave ones, who were the first to take male or female form as we know it, were the earliest Atlanteans. An extraordinary new divine quest was under way. The eternal longing of every human to find his or her other half began.

Earth was unique. It was the only place in the universes where Source was conducting this particular trial; the one location where spirits could incarnate in a physical body to experience all the senses, as well as emotions and sexuality. It was an amazing opportunity, never before envisaged. These souls would have to learn to manage, support and nurture their physical forms, as well as Gaia, the Earth. Furthermore, the essence of their soul would build their skeleton or frame, while their thoughts would create and form their body of flesh. Thus, they were totally responsible for their bodies and their lives. The aim was now to discover whether divine sparks could live a full physical life, while maintaining their connection with the Source.

Those who incarnated into Atlantis were genetically encoded to be tall and well-built with blond hair and blue eyes. But Atlantis was only one of several experiments taking place on Earth. In diverse parts of the planet, various races with different genetic coding had other tasks to fulfil. One of the direct results of this is that we now have on Earth a contrast of cultures who do not understand each other.

Almost everyone on Earth has had an incarnation in Atlantis, where great spiritual and technological knowledge was amassed beyond anything we can currently comprehend. It is now time for the ancient wisdom to be brought forward so that another Golden Age can develop.

Atlantis became the longest and greatest civilisation on Earth and lasted from 250,000 BC to 10,000 BC. During this period, the Intergalactic Council terminated the test several times. On the first and second occasions, the people lost their connection with their divinity and descended into bestiality and the use of black magic. As no progress had been made during these first two attempts, for the third experiment, the Intergalactic Council decided to repopulate Atlantis differently. This time they prepared the continent as a veritable cornucopia of delight. Settlers were invited from the universes and everything was given to them. Homes, temples and all that they could need or want awaited them. They brought amazing technological and psychic skills with them and had very little to learn. At first they were totally cosseted and within a relatively short time the new arrivals divided into two camps. Some became lazy, hedonistic and grasping. They were known as the Sons of Belial and sought physical and sensual gratification of every description. Greed, lust, envy, gluttony and violence became their driving force. These were the people who originated the concept of the seven deadly sins. The Children of the Law of One, on the other hand, sought to maintain their connection with the Divine. Knowing that their purpose was to remain one with God, they focused on love, light, balance, purity, justice and cosmic wisdom. The schism between the two factions inevitably led to conflict and, despite being given so much, disharmony arose.

Another problem occurred during this epoch. As a result of evolution, animals became huge and giant elephants, mammoths, massive cats, enormous horses, mastodon, vast komodo dragons and birds started to overrun the planet. Masterminded by an entity from another world, they became very aggressive. This made life on the surface very difficult and the people tried all peaceful methods to control the animals without success. Eventually a five-nation conference was organised to discuss the situation. Using the powers that were available to them, delegates teleported from Russia, Sudan, India and Peru to Atlantis. Such was their desperation that they resolved to create a series of nuclear bombs, which they hoped would kill the beasts. We no longer understand the exact make-up of these bombs, but in 52,000 BC they were detonated underground resulting in massive earthquakes, the repercussions of which caused the creatures to perish. However, it also upset the balance of nature and the people could not survive either. So the inhabitants of Earth died and their spirits returned to their home planets. As a consequence of this disruption, in 50,000 BC the Earth shifted on its axis and Atlantis became five islands.

In 28,000 BC the Intergalactic Council met and in their wisdom decided once more to re-seed Atlantis with physical beings: men, women and animals. Again, an invitation was sent to the universes and beings arrived from many other planets and galaxies, most of which are unknown to humans today. Only a few of them were the spirits of the Lemurians who originally populated Earth.

This time the Council decided that it was not helpful to make life for the volunteers so comfortable when they arrived. The people came in with all the practical and psychic skills they would need in place, but their homes and temples were not built for them. They had to create their own and this joint undertaking bonded them for a short while. Priests, who had been specially trained in preparation for this challenge had advanced know-ledge with which to help the volunteers. However, this venture deteriorated in the same way as its predecessors. The Children of the Law of One sought to maintain their divine connections, but the Sons of Belial, who had returned to incarnation, became much stronger than the pure ones. These people had become disconnected from their hearts, and used technology and black occult power to disempower and control the masses. Warmongers proliferated.

Many of these Sons of Belial have subsequently reincarnated.

Hitler, Genghis Khan and Mussolini were three of them; Saddam Hussein is another. Throughout history, other Sons of Belial have continued to return to Earth and often remain in the background influencing spiritually weak leaders. This is happening even now.

The fourth experiment ran for 10,000 years until 18,000 BC when the Intergalactic Council decided that, because of the gross misuse of power, Atlantis must end again. They chose to move the Earth's magnetic pole, using the instrument of a comet to facilitate an abrupt termination. This created an ice age, which was a form of purification for the planet. The landmass was reshaped once more and the five islands of Atlantis now became significantly smaller, with only the high places remaining, to form a chain of islands linking to North America.

As soon as the previous age ended, the Intergalactic Council started to plan an entirely new phase of Atlantis. While they deliberated for a period of 2,000 years, the planet was cleansed and detoxified by the ice age. Atlantis had become much smaller and it clustered in the centre of what we now know as the Atlantic Ocean. Bermuda, the Canary Islands and the Azores are a few of the remaining parts of the great continent. Lanzarote was also a physical part of it, but was never peopled as part of the project.

Despite previous aborted attempts, the Council had high hopes that this time the new immigrants to Earth would maintain purity and a high level of spirituality – for, having learnt from the previous experiments, this one was to be set up in a different way. The Intergalactic Council decided that to enable the purity of the mission to be maintained the area containing Atlantis must be set apart and protected. This would also mean that the new possibilities could be tested in a controlled environment.

At last the plan for the Golden Age was put into place. First the Intergalactic Council built the Temple of Poseidon, sometimes known as the Cathedral of the Sacred Heights, which contained the Great Crystal, the generator crystal of Atlantis. The Temple was created in the cradle of the Atlas Mountains and formed a seventh peak. These peaks symbolised the Seven Pillars of the Universe, which are the Seven Spiritual Laws or cosmic energies that govern humanity. These are:

The Law of One. This is represented by the great Temple itself in the centre of Atlantis and affirms that there is no separation from God. It proclaims we are all part of the whole and our actions affect every single creature throughout the universes. For example, when a polar bear sneezes in the Arctic, a grain of sand moves in the Sahara.

The Law of Karma. There is a spiritual working out for all things, though it may take lifetimes. Thoughts, words and actions are all energies that come back to you in the exact measure at which you give them out. Ultimately: as you give, so you receive.

The Law of Manifestation. Like attracts like. Your thoughts, words and deeds attract like to them and can draw material things, people and experiences into your physical life. You are the power that creates everything in your life.

The Law of Grace. Unconditional love, forgiveness and compassion offer grace, which dissolves karma and accrues blessings.

The Law of Responsibility. When you take responsibility for your thoughts, words and actions, you take mastery of your life. You are then able to respond appropriately to all that you experience.

The Law of Unconditional Love. Unconditional love is a state of acceptance and non-attachment, which forms no emotional strings. When you love in this way you set yourself and others free.

The Law of Intention. The moment you gain clarity you can take decisions. This moves the universal energy to assist you and you can progress with strength. If your intention is pure, you earn no karma, whatever the outcome. For example, if you are expanding your business with the intention of bringing help to dis-advantaged people, but some employees are unfortunately made redundant, it does not weigh against you. On the other hand, if you are sacking people careless of their misfortune and for the sole purpose of excessive personal gain, you will bear karma when your soul is ready to do so.

The Seven Pillars of the Universe
(The Seven Spiritual Laws)

The Intergalactic Council were the architects of Atlantis. They worked through twelve highly evolved souls, the High Priests and Priestesses, who took physical bodies that vibrated between the fifth- and sixth-dimensional frequency. They were collectively known as the Alta and were the master builders, who took all the practical earthly decisions about the setting up of the continent while taking general instruction from the Council. For example, they channelled the spiritual laws for Earth through Thoth, who was one of the High Priests of Atlantis and was later worshipped as a god in Egypt. Atlantis was divided into twelve regions, each one governed by one of the Alta, so naturally each had a different focus. In the earliest days of the golden times, only these twelve great Initiates could enter the Temple of Poseidon; later they initiated others.

At the start of this final experiment, the volunteers arrived as strangers to each other, in bodies, which they had never before experienced. This time the Intergalactic Council realised that, if the volunteers to Earth were going to maintain their divine connection and learn from being in a body, they would have to co-operate, share and work together. This would help them to maintain a high frequency. So only water, earth, plants and trees awaited them. Nothing else was prepared. For 1,500 years, during the golden period, the Intergalactic Council and the Illumined Ones throughout the universes watched with awe as those incarnate in Atlantis maintained divine simplicity, performed incredible technological feats and developed wondrous spiritual powers. These settlers from all over the universes brought heaven to Earth and created the highest spiritual time there has ever been on this planet.

However, eventually history repeated itself. Control, lust, cruelty and greed overtook most of the people. Despite many attempts on the part of the Council to help the planet, at last a decision was taken to terminate the Atlantean experiment for the final time. In approximately 10,000 BC, Poseidon, High Priest of Atlantis and God of the Seas, declared that Atlantis must be flooded, an event recorded in the Bible and other literature of the world. The great continent finally disappeared under the waves. Some spirits returned to their homes but those who caused the destruction were inevitably tied to Earth until they redeemed their karma.

The High Priests and Priestesses, who later became mythical Gods in Egypt and Greece, led those members of their tribes who were pure and willing, to various parts of the world that had been specially prepared for them. We discuss this later in the book. By breeding with local people in their new areas they were to maintain the genetic wisdom of Atlantis on Earth.

12,000 years later, we have once more devolved to the depths of human degradation. For aeons the planet has been so dark and heavy that the Intergalactic Council could not reach us without doing great damage, which they were reluctant to do. Now, at last, humans are looking towards the spiritual, with resulting upheaval and turmoil as the shadow of humanity is released. The planet is becoming lighter and the angelic forces and higher beings can connect with many of us once more.

The incredible spiritual wisdom and technological knowledge of pure Atlantis has been recorded and stored. Many of these great ones are now returning into incarnation at the start of the Aquarian Age to facilitate the return of the energy of pure Atlantis. It is time now for those who are ready to access and bring back this light, and to enable the energy of the golden times to return.

CHAPTER 2

The Early Days

At the start of the Golden Age of Atlantis, once the Temple of Poseidon was completed, the Intergalactic Council sent out an invitation to the whole cosmos inviting souls to incarnate and take part in the latest experiment.

Souls responded from many star systems and universes, and the High Priests and Priestesses – the rulers of the twelve tribes – chose beings with specific energies for the individual regions. These Atlanteans did not look as we look, for they carried a higher light, which they radiated, so there was an ethereal quality about them. Nor did the original population birth through human mothers. They teleported or came in space ships and in ways that we do not yet understand.

Like all beings who incarnate, they had to go through the Veil of Amnesia, forgetting their divine origins. This is part of the curriculum for anyone coming to Earth and it must have been extremely difficult for people arriving in adult bodies, without the support, love and teaching that parents offer to new babies.

The Intergalactic Council watched with interest as this last experiment took place. Having taken on physical form with all human needs and wants, could spirit master desire? Could these people still maintain their oneness with All That Is? Could they live in peace, co-operation and harmony? In the early days, the volunteers chosen were all at the top of the fifth dimensional frequency range. Would this make a difference?

7,000 people incarnated into each of the tribes; 84,000 souls in all of which approximately half were male and half female. They were genetically encoded to walk, talk, eat and to perform human functions and certain basic skills, which they had to practise and develop. Individuals also had twelve strands of DNA. It has only been since the fall of Atlantis that we have been reduced to two strands of DNA. Much information remains latent within us, to be restored when we are ready. How strange it must have felt for those in this first phase for, of course, their spirits had never before been encased in a physical form.

Initially the newcomers were given something akin to a huge, silk marquee for shelter and some food and basic clothing. Together, they set out to build camps then solid structures for their homes. They started to grow and gather food. From the beginning they all pooled their talents for the common good. The plan was cleverly devised in this way by the Intergalactic Council to encourage people to work together. In co-operating for their common survival they created community and it was because they had a vision for the highest good that the frequency remained so steadfast. They were not given the right to an idyllic lifestyle. They had to earn this by following the spiritual laws that governed this planet. However, at that time, it was easier for people to create Heaven on Earth than it is now because they arrived here free of karma.

Just as now, no human walked alone. Guardian angels were appointed by Source to look after each individual and act as a messenger and intermediary with the Godhead. These angels held the divine blueprint for the life mission of their charges. Because the frequency of the people was so high, the guardian angels of that time had a similar frequency to the archangels who help humans in current times.

The land prepared for the people was abundantly wooded. Rivers rushed down from the mountains and crisscrossed the plains, giving pure water for drinking and bathing. The soil was very rich and fertile, and the grass was lush and green. Edible plants would be gathered readily and they intuitively knew which ones served their purpose. They also intrinsically understood how to make beverages, for example using herbs for teas. The premise followed by the Intergalactic Council was that if the newcomers needed something in order to survive the information would rise to consciousness. The weather was clement everywhere but it varied across the five islands, being cooler in the north than the south.

The early settlers had to start by building dwellings from the natural materials available and by organising their communities. Of course, they had to create furniture, cooking pots, clothing and even pathways, but their first priority was to build temples. Each of the twelve tribes built a simple house of worship; really a place of thanksgiving. Every evening, when their work of building and creating was complete, they went to the temple to give thanks for the opportunity and the divine munificence. They lived totally in the moment, joyously celebrating all that they had, with no concept of tomorrow.

The focal point of each temple was a crystal. These connected to each other as well as to the magnificent generator crystal in the Temple of Poseidon. Because running water brought them peace and harmony, they soon built fountains in these places of thanksgiving. Later, the buildings were used for education, as well as community centres, where social gatherings took place. The Atlanteans of this period also loved to give thanks out in nature, to the Divine. They built stone circles, with a predetermined link to a star, through which they could draw in wisdom and knowledge from the galaxies. All the stars of their origin were honoured and their energies were linked in this way to Earth.

Animals

At first there were no animals, but soon after the humans inhabited Atlantis, animals incarnated, starting with those who offered themselves in service, such as cows, goats, sheep, horses and other beasts of burden. All the early Atlanteans were vegetarian, though they accepted the produce of animals. Humans linked telepathically, as well as verbally, with these animals and asked permission to sit on the horses, which they learnt to ride bareback. They accepted milk from cows and goats, wool from sheep, and eggs from hens. All this involved communication and helped to develop community. After the service animals arrived in Atlantis, cats, dogs and other domestic animals followed, as well as wild ones. They were all creatures who wished to take part in this most extraordinary intergalactic opportunity for spiritual development.

Spiritual and Psychic Gifts

Each person had psychic gifts like clairvoyance, clairaudience, clairsentience, healing and telepathy. However, other gifts such as teleportation, mind control, telekinesis and levitation had to be developed. The rulers decided that if the early settlers of this Golden Age were to arrive with all their gifts of power in place, the foundation for co-operation would be missing. It is exactly the same in current times. A baby is born genetically encoded with gifts it has acquired over lifetimes in this and other star systems. These talents have to be practised, worked on and developed: a gifted musician has to practise to become a maestro, a born gardener has to learn about how to work with his plants.

Emotions and Sexuality

The people were not only learning to survive in completely uncharted territory, they also had to develop and integrate their emotions and their sexuality – two aspects that none of these newcomers to Earth had ever experienced. One more challenge was the instinctive longing to seek their soul mate, which was encoded into the DNA of humans when the androgynous Lemurians decided to split into masculine and feminine bodies. From that moment humans quested to find the other aspect of them: their twin flame.

In current times, humanity has sunk down to a third-dimensional frequency, where sexuality is often based on sensation and need. Today, the experience of orgasm offers a moment in the now and is often the nearest a person gets to the bliss of connection with God. In the early days of Atlantis, when the settlers vibrated at a fifth-dimensional frequency, the people were not interested in sex without love. They sought only a soul mate – one who resonated deeply with them at emotional, mental, spiritual, as well as physical levels. The sexual expression of love was not only a merging of their auric fields, but it also enabled them to complete their lost wholeness.

Experiencing the Senses

Those courageous early adventurers had undertaken a mighty task. Arriving in alien territory, peopled by strangers from various planetary systems, they were expected to work in co-operation with all the different beings and learn to relate with them all to create a new community. They had to do this while maintaining harmony and the highest integrity, and at the same time they were to act with peace, love, joy and gratitude.

These newcomers really did appreciate their amazing good fortune at being chosen from trillions of volunteers to experience life in a human body. Imagine their awe each morning as the sun rose in its full glory and sailed across the blue sky. They watched, with joy, the energy fields of every living thing, radiating and pulsing in the clear air. They listened rapturously to the song of birds, the chirrup of a cricket or the rustle of leaves. They would stroke a leaf or run their fingers through cool running water and rejoice in the sensation. When they touched the warm, moist earth they could smell its rich smell and they would marvel at the sweet fragrance of a flower. For the first time they could hear the voice of a friend and feel the emotion of love flooding their hearts. They could cuddle or hug another being in the flesh and feel his or her warmth and closeness. To them, it was extraordinary and filled them with wonder. Something as simple as eating a banana allowed them to see, touch, smell and taste, so they constantly felt blessed to be allowed the opportunity of incarnation. Throughout the universes, angels and spirits, high and low, have longed for these experiences. Even now, we who have been here many times appreciate the unique wonders of Earth, such as a glorious sunset or the smell of a flower, for all who incarnate are genetically encoded to do so. The early inhabitants of Atlantis who had never been here before were even more profoundly affected.

Our current world is so full of noise that we can no longer find silence, but the land at that time was still and quiet, and the people were filled with a sense of deep peace. They learned that if they breathed slowly they could maintain this sense of serenity and savour everything in their new world.

Rulers of Atlantis

The High Priests and Priestesses were originally the benefactors of the people, providing them with their survival needs, food, shelter and clothing, until they could create their own. When they were self-sufficient, the Great Initiates focused on teaching them about the power of crystals and how to use them. The next part of their training was awesome, if they wished to undertake it. It involved mind control, which enabled them to practise levitation, telekinesis, teleportation and the ability to manifest. Their tuition encompassed the use of the frequencies of sound and light.

Eventually, if they attained the status of Magi, they were taught to fly and communicate with other galaxies. During this fifth experiment, the Intergalactic Council introduced technology slowly. Information was genetically encoded into the High Priests and Priestesses and when it was believed that the people were ready for another level of learning they would discuss it with the Council before showing it to their charges.

There were various levels of priesthood: High Priest and Priestess, Mage, Initiate, Adept and Novice. The most highly evolved of course, were the High Priests and Priestesses, who liased with the Intergalactic Council and communicated with the Magi and the Initiates. Initially, the rulers had a duty to look out for those who had the potential to become spiritual lights in their own right and who would succeed them. For this they sought those who exhibited the qualities of leadership and pure spirituality. They also selected people who demonstrated the various aptitudes required for the golden future of Atlantis. Management and organisational skills were paramount not only in these early days, but throughout this whole period of history. They needed people to oversee cultural affairs, building design, teaching, healing and many other aspects of life.

We cannot underestimate the training the first group had to go through or the work they had to undertake to prepare Atlantis – not only for them, but for the generations to follow. However, those original residents of Golden Atlantis have now evolved into mighty beings in their own right. Many of them returned to the star of their soul origin, taking their new higher understandings and wisdom with them. This they taught to the beings on their home planets, thus spreading the energy of pure Atlantis through the galaxies.

A similar challenge and opportunity is being offered to every single person who has incarnated into Earth at this present time. The chances for spiritual promotion are greater now than they have ever been.

EXERCISE: *Back to Basics*

This is an invitation to go back to basics: to experience the essence of being in a body. Imagine you are one of the early Atlanteans and this is your first visit to Earth. Go outside and perceive Earth with the senses of a stranger in a foreign place. For example, go to different trees and feel the bark with your fingertips, pick up a pebble or stone and stroke it or be totally still and listen to the sound of the birds.

CHAPTER 3

Birth, Marriage and Death in Atlantis

Once the original volunteers to this phase of Atlantis had learnt how to meet their survival needs by creating community through co-operation, more souls were invited to populate the continent. They, however, needed to be birthed through the physical body and looked after during babyhood and childhood. To undertake this responsibility, couples came together in a committed, blessed union. No ring or other symbol was exchanged, for they considered no one could own or limit another in this place of free will. The union was for mutual caring, learning and comfort. At that time no one had sex outside a relationship, because the commitment of birthing and caring for the future generations was considered sacred.

Before a marriage was sanctioned, a priest examined the auras of eligible couples to check that they were spiritually and emotionally compatible. This was to ensure that a baby received a balanced emotional upbringing, exposed to both masculine and feminine energy in its formative years. Throughout the universes, beings watched what was happening here. Would sex corrupt or would it remain a beautiful, transcendent experience that enriched the lives of the couple and brought them closer? Those who observed the inhabitants of Atlantis handling relationships, sexuality, birth and death with integrity, saw that it provided many challenges and a rich opportunity for learning and growth. Incarnation into a physical body was viewed as the Everest of challenges. Then, as now, souls queued up to undertake the experience.

In early Atlantis, when a couple decided that they were ready for the responsibility of parenthood they would discuss what sort of soul they were best able to serve as parents. They would then consciously communicate with the spirit of one of the volunteers who fitted their criteria. The energy created in the act of lovemaking drew this particular being to them and a spiritual commitment was then made to start the physicality of pregnancy within the womb of the mother. In current times, the same method of soul choice takes place, but the decisions are usually taken out of conscious awareness. In Atlantis, every single baby was consciously chosen, invited, welcomed and loved.

Moving On

When the original 84,000 souls entered Atlantis, the vast majority were destined to become part of a couple. However, the Intergalactic Council was aware that trauma and emotional destruction within relationships had often been a problem in the earlier experiments. So this time a number of entrants came with the specific purpose of remaining single. The intention was that they would stay free, forming a nucleus of emotionally-clear counsellors and guides. Many of these trained as novices, the first level of priesthood, while other single adults looked after those who were orphaned.

At this stage of Atlantis, people only died if they had preagreed to leave the experiment in order that others could experience the emotions surrounding separation and bereavement. Even in our times, death is a predetermined choice made by the soul. We still choose, consciously or unconsciously, our method of passing, often for the spiritual growth of the family and sometimes as a wake-up call for our loved ones. At other times people decide, at a soul level, to die more slowly in a way that will give those around them a chance to adjust emotionally to their impending departure.

In Atlantis, as now, many souls exited this physical plane because it was time for them to take part in another piece of light work. Perhaps the Higher Self of one person may have agreed to help a grandchild or great-grandchild, from the spiritual realms, as they made their incarnation. Or there may have been teaching or healing work to do on another galaxy. Also, as now, there were always those who had not fulfilled their intentions on Earth and needed guidance and counselling while they are asleep. During sleep, our spirits leave our physical bodies and travel to other planes for spiritual help. They may be offered help to enable them to decide the next step on their spiritual journey, for we are all on a journey back to the Godhead. In Atlantis, as now, they did not lose someone when a person died. They had simply stepped into another room of the mansion of the Infinite, and then, as now, they would, meet again if they wished to.

Community Life

After the original phase of communal survival, the next learning was about creating family life within community. When a couple committed to a union, they built their own home and everyone helped, freely contributing their time, skills and ideas. They constructed the houses out of natural materials, wood, straw, mud and anything available in their areas.

Karma was not created because no one ever gave without receiving or received without giving. This fostered selflessness, appreciation, creativity, generosity, respect and all the higher qualities required in such a community. There was no ownership. It was deemed that ownership promoted difference, separation and greed, while the cosmic experiment was designed to establish sharing, caring, trust and oneness.

Everyone was encouraged to do what he or she loved best. The farmers worked together, so did the furniture makers, the bakers, the cooks, the builders, seamstresses and all other skill groups. They placed their product in a collective pool to be used as needed. Money simply did not exist at this time.

The first babies who incarnated were regarded with wonder and respect. They were cherished and deeply loved by everyone, for they belonged to the community. However, it was their parents who met their immediate physical and emotional needs. Because both parents and baby were telepathic, they would communicate mind to mind and this meant that the parents automatically perceived the needs of the child. They watched for, and helped to hone, the child's latent abilities. The community helped to serve each baby's social and educational needs. When they were quite small the children spent part of the day in a nursery, where they were cared for and helped to develop socially and spiritually by people who were chosen for their qualities of love, caring and wisdom, and their ability to teach babies and children. Trained priests helped to maintain the spiritual energy of these crèches.

Education and Development

The priests assessed each child according to the spiritual and psychic gifts he or she brought into Atlantis, and drew out these talents. Even as babies these new entrants were encouraged to develop and express that which they could do well. As a result they grew up with a sense of self-worth, happiness, belonging and connection. They were nurtured so that they could grow into balanced, loving adults. This created an inclusive society where no one experienced isolation or loneliness. When they were ready, as young as three years of age, the children were gathered into groups for education. This took place outside, in nature, where they were encouraged to express their creativity and learn through song, drama, music, art and play. The aim was to expand their right brain, which keeps the connection to Source open. Their psychic abilities were also encouraged and directed.

The priesthood was made up of men and women. At the age of seven, the children were taken by them to the temples to be taught. The classes were light and fun-filled, for the teachers realised that the young ones needed their childhood and must not be made to grow up too quickly. The first qualities to be developed within the children were awareness and respect. The youngsters learnt to be in touch with everything in their environment and to watch the energies of plants, animals, people and all things, so they knew if a plant or animal needed help. They could sense the needs and feelings of all around them and, because everything was regarded as an extension of self, they knew at a cellular level that they could not hurt anything without hurting themselves. Being psychically open, they could see the energies within and around everything, right down to the subatomic level. Even the youngest child could see auras. Consequently, there were no secrets, which meant it was safe for people to keep their hearts open, so there was no guilt, shame, resentment, fear or anger. Openness, peace, love, joy, innocence and trust created safe welcoming communities.

The High Priests and Priestesses were given information from the Intergalactic Council about their perception of the perfect education for the children. This was passed down to the priest teachers and proved flexible enough to allow for individuality, so they continued to use these guidelines for future generations.

At school, the children's spiritual and psychic gifts were not just encouraged but were carefully developed. They were taught self-discipline and elementary mind control. If, for example, a child was hungry and wanted an apple from a tree, he could simply focus on the fruit with his mind and it would float to him. This development of their psychic gifts conferred immense power and responsibility on the youngsters and helped them to grow spiritually.

Because the children were safe and secure, and trusted their environment, they were able to truly relax both body and mind so that they were receptive to the cosmic information the priest was imparting to them. The priests taught telepathically so that it was easier for the pupils to absorb information. If a child found it difficult to grasp a cosmic concept, the priest would pour pure white light into his or her mind, relaxing every cell even more deeply, and then the understanding could be received and accepted more easily. Music was used in the temple to assist the children to go into a state of relaxation. While they were in trance the Atlanteans practised visualisation. As this is one of the first steps towards manifestation, it was important that even children learnt this skill. We will give you much more information about the powers they developed later in the book.

Health

As part of keeping everything in balance and harmony, emotions were immediately addressed and honoured, which meant that there were no underlying grievances or issues. Therefore, people were happy and healthy, and children were brought up within contented families.

The Intergalactic Council was very aware of the frailties of the human body. One of the first dedicated areas within each temple was for healing. Family members would regularly visit the temples for a check up, during which the priests would balance and realign each person's mental, emotional and spiritual bodies using sound and crystals, so that they maintained optimum health. As a result, in the earliest days, there was no illness. In the event of an accident or trauma that knocked someone off centre within their aura, the priests would offer deeper healing.

There was a keen emphasis on family life and extended families loved to spend most of their time outside, picnicking together and having fun in nature. The children responded to the simplicity of life, playing round the clusters of natural, ecological homes, surrounded by greenery and trees. They also swam and frolicked in the water of streams, lakes and fountains. As the first babies grew into children, animals arrived in Atlantis to help with work, offer their produce and enhance family life.

EXERCISE: *The Humming Ball*

This is one of the simplest and most effective ways of sending your higher energy and love to another person. You can use it to heal relationships, or to bathe someone in love, abundance, prosperity, wisdom or any other gift. It is so effective that we have known physical healing to take place when a humming ball, sent with love, was received. One young man projected a healing humming ball from a workshop to his depressed mother. Although she did not know consciously what was happening, she actually saw the ball enter her room as a golden light. The depression lifted and has never returned.

Like meditations or invocations this exercise opens you up. You always need to close down, as indicated, at the end.

1. Sit quietly, on your own or with others, and decide where you wish to send the energy and what quality you wish to send.
2. Place your hands in front of you as if they were holding a ball.
3. Ask the angels to work with you.
4. Focus on seeing the quality that you wish to send filling the ball you are holding. As you do so, hum softly and imagine a colour expanding the ball.
5. When your humming ball is vibrating with the qualities and love you wish to offer, picture the person to whom you are

projecting it, and imagine them receiving it. (You can also mentally throw humming balls to places, situations or people you have never met.)

6. Close down by touching each chakra in turn, and placing a cross or other symbol of protection that is meaningful to you, over them.

CHAPTER 4

Animals in Atlantis

The Intergalactic Council wanted to be sure that the settlers, in their physical bodies, fully understood and honoured the divinity of all things. They were pleased that people asked the plants if they could pick their fruit and, in exchange for this bounty, sang to them or cleared the weeds that choked their roots. People would even ask the permission of the weeds before they pulled them from the earth. If a branch needed to be cut from a tree, Atlanteans would first explain what they were about to do, to the tree, so that it could withdraw its energy from the limb. This could then be severed without pain. They would talk to the elementals within crystals and these would gladly work with them. They asked leave from the water spirits to enter a river and in exchange were kept safe. At all times they respected and were sensitive to the vibrations of all life forms.

Service Animals

When the original volunteers had settled, the Council arranged for animals to arrive in Atlantis. First came the service animals: horses, cows, goats, deer, sheep, bees and chicken. Their soul purpose in taking part in the experiment of Atlantis was the same as for humans. Could their spirits incarnate in a body of flesh and still maintain their divinity? Could they unconditionally love humans and each other within the confines of a physical body and the challenges of Earth? At first it was relatively easy. Humans and animals honoured and served each other: people were deeply grateful to the animals for providing them with produce and in return they gave them food and shelter, loved them, and let them be free.

COWS

Cows descended from Lakuma, one of the stars round Sirius and of a vibration much higher than we can currently tune into, which is why it is invisible to us as yet. Their service was to offer milk. They were also learning to develop the qualities of being earthed, steady, stable, solid, reliable, and gentle – and, of course, they demonstrated a wonderful capacity for giving. They expressed extreme opposites of masculine and feminine energy: the cow being nurturing and loving: the bull, powerful and protective.

In recent times, when the herds allowed mad cow disease to enter their systems they were demonstrating to humans that we need them more than they need us. Surrendering themselves to be sacrificed on flaming funeral pyres was a way of drawing attention to this. The flames also helped to purify some of the vibrations of pain and suffering we humans have inflicted on cattle over many thousands of years. But in the early days of Atlantis, cows lived in harmony with the people, who treated them as part of the family. They gave and received true love.

HORSES

Horses also came from Lakuma. They are highly-evolved beings and they offered themselves in supportive roles for the humans who were undertaking the Atlantis experiment. They were used as a mode of transport and were ridden without saddles or bridles. The rider would sit bareback, hold the mane of the horse for balance and directions were given telepathically. There was a huge bond of love between these beautiful creatures and humans. Horses demonstrated qualities of dignity, self-worth, honour and love, and many of them still radiate these qualities. It was not until the vibration of Atlantis started to decline that they were harnessed, saddled and ridden in races for money.

DEER
These sweet, gentle animals, which also came from Lakuma, were nervous, watchful and wary. They arrived to learn about trust and they are still teaching us about trust now. If you see a deer, it suggests you need to trust more or at least look at your trust levels.

CHICKENS
Hens came to Earth from a distant planet of another universe, which is unknown to us. Their service was to offer eggs and feathers. In the early days all the other energies were slow, languid and peaceful. Hens offered the balance, which was liveliness, activity and quickness. Into a world of being, they demonstrated doing. They were learning to live, serve and offer themselves.

GOATS
Goats came to offer milk and were waste-disposal experts. They incarnated from Orion, which is the spiritual university of this galaxy, and offered lessons of enlightenment.

SHEEP
Among the first service animals to flock here were sheep, who came from the Pleiades, offering wool, comfort and a sense of goodwill.

BEES
Also from the Pleiades, bees came to learn about the sweetness of life and to bring us honey. They served to pollinate flowers and demonstrated method, order and aspects of sacred geometry. And, of course, in those early days they did not need stings.

When those animals who came in direct service to humans had settled on Earth, the Intergalactic Council sent domestic animals.

Domestic Animals

DOGS

Dogs were all the same breed, just different colours; the nearest equivalent we have now are lurchers. Their main role was to be with children, who learnt to understand about responsibility for others, as they considered the needs of their pet, and how to care for and empathise with other creatures. In turn the dog would experience life with humans. Its purpose was to learn to nurture children and to keep them safe from accidents. When a child was born, a dog would be attracted to the child's energy and would turn up at the house. Parents would expect a dog to arrive for their child and one day they would open the door and find it there. Every child had a dog and the average family was three children, so there would be at least three dogs in each household. Children and their dogs experienced companionship and it was a symbiotic relationship on every level. The dog even went to school with the child.

The natural life span of a dog was thirteen to sixteen years, equivalent to the childhood of its human companion. At the end of this time, the human either took a partner or moved to a single person's accommodation to train to become a priest or for another vocation. When this happened, both dog and human knew they had served each other and that their purpose together was done. Their energies would then separate, the dog would pass over and its spirit would return to its home planet of Canis Major.

After the decline of Atlantis, however, humans started to breed dogs for their own selfish purposes.

CATS

Cats are enlightened and independent beings. They are the one species who came to Earth so evolved that they had nothing to learn from humans and consequently they did not need us. They came from Orion, the great spiritual planet, which is why their energy was so pure. Even today they are highly independent. In the early days all cats were black and very 'Egyptian-looking'. Black is, of course, the colour of deep mystery and sacred arts. It is the ultimate feminine vibration.

A cat went to every home to help maintain a pure energy there. In later days their mission was to try to raise the energy in the house. Felines at this golden time were vegetarian, like all high frequency creatures, and allowed themselves to be fed by humans. They did not need claws to catch or kill prey, but they loved to climb trees and had a great affinity with them. At the temples people were employed specifically to look after their needs and they were very much revered. They were used in temples because their psychic ability was so high, so they partici-pated in rituals, and ceremonies and added their energies where they were needed.

Healers always had a cat to boost the power. If a crystal arrange-ment that was being used for healing was slightly out of alignment, the cat would adjust it, making sure the crystals offered the optimum healing. Cats were always present at deaths too. In those days the spirit often needed to be guided, so their cat travelled out of body to accompany them and make sure they did not get lost.

The Magi also had cats. Hundreds of years later when the pure ones first had a sense of things going wrong in Atlantis, they sent to Orion for more cats to help hold the light on Earth. In pure Atlantis, there were, of course, no entities or dark thought forms, but later in the devolved times cats would watch over their families and protect them from entities. They still do this, trying to guard their owners and the planet.

RABBITS

The third domestic animal was the rabbit. Like dogs, they were protectors of children, as well as their playmates. Dogs took their jobs as guardians very seriously and, with their loving, no-nonsense approach, helped the child to develop its masculine nature. In balance, the rabbit offered feminine energy, and was light, fun and fluffy. A child went to its rabbit for comfort if it felt hurt, for they help to heal the heart.

Dogs and rabbits provided the protector and carer roles for the children, who loved them both dearly. The dog went to school with his charge and the rabbit maintained the energy at home. Like cats, the rabbits came from Orion and it was not unusual to see cats and rabbits conversing, as they knew they came from the same place but had been allocated different jobs. The cats were regal and knew they were boss, whereas rabbits were practical and helpful.

Other Creatures

PIGS

Pigs also arrived in the second wave, from the Pleiades. They came, as part of the ecological balance to eat the leftovers. Like hens, they were at that time quick and active, and were also valued for their intelligence and wisdom. They did not live as part of the household, but offered friendship, love and care to humans.

BIRDS

A whole variety of birds incarnated from Sirius to learn about mastering gravity and to maintain their inherent qualities, while fettered by a physical body. They came to teach serenity, dignity and calmness, and to act as a reminder of freedom to earthbound beings. Brightly coloured birds constantly delighted the people with their song, their beautiful plumage and message of freedom.

Swans were especially admired and honoured in Atlantis for their composure, regal qualities and peace. They have manifestly demonstrated their life purpose and even now are considered royal birds. All pure white creatures vibrate at a very high frequency.

FISH

Fish volunteered to come to Earth from the constellation Pisces and their task was ecological. They were to keep the seas and rivers clean.

RED SQUIRRELS

Red squirrels were beautiful, highly-evolved and wise creatures from Orion, bringing freedom and a sense of joy and liveliness.

RATS AND MICE

These were not sent in golden times, but eventually, as Atlantis devolved, rats and mice arrived to clear rubbish on the planet. Rats were more aggressive and scavenged, whereas the mice had a gentler energy that took advantage of situations that presented themselves.

DOLPHINS

Dolphins, the wise ones of the planet, brought their high energy, wisdom and knowledge from Sirius. They are the keepers of cosmic knowledge, holding the information like a computer. In the days of telepathy, they were the internet to which humans turned to access knowledge.

The dolphins incarnated as teachers. They were the psychics: High Priests and Priestesses of the oceans, who maintained the vibration of the waters. The people of Atlantis built huge pools for the dolphins, and swam with them, telepathically receiving guidance, information and wisdom.

When Atlantis began to fall, the Intergalactic Council decided to sweep back the sacred ancient knowledge and wisdom, and downloaded the information to the dolphins. When Atlantis finally disintegrated, certain of those who orchestrated its destruction took dolphin bodies. Every detail of what happened was recorded and the Intergalactic Council use these dolphins as a memory base to access why and how it fell.

The Sphinx holds all the information pertaining to our planet as a whole, not just Atlantis, of all that has ever been, is, and will be. It has always done so. The angel dolphins and master crystal skull, discussed in Chapter 25, maintain all the wisdom of Atlantis. But the Council wanted to be absolutely certain that the data would be preserved and so individual files were sent out to be preserved by different beings. Different kinds of dolphins each keep one twelfth of the information, as do the individual crystal skulls.

Animals from Other Experiments

Other animals were not included in Atlantis. Elephants, giraffes and camels, for example, incarnated into Africa as part of a different experiment, and crocodiles and marsupials came into Australia as part of a galactic test there.

Lions, tigers, leopards and other large felines were also part of a different venture on Earth and were even more highly evolved and regal than the black cats. When Atlantis was declining, the Intergalactic Council sent more 'powerful' help to the continent. They brought the big cats through the energy biosphere surrounding the experiment, so that their incredible frequency could be used. Later, in Egypt, the big cats worked with the Pharoahs, who were not as pure as the Atlanteans and needed greater support.

Astral entities

MOSQUITOES

Mosquitoes are not divine creatures, they are astral entities. People send out thoughts all the time. In low-frequency times, when humans were intensely irritated they projected their anger and frustration powerfully out into the ethers. This eventually became a thought form, which materialised into matter and the mosquito was born. Like all dark forces, mosquitoes continue to serve us by rousing our irritation or by being attracted to us when we are annoyed.

FLIES

Flies are also astral entities, created by the buzzing, angry thought forms of humans. They are the downside of a human's power to co-create with the Divine. Once Atlantis fell, the world started opening up and people travelled. The ecological principles that had been developed in pure Atlantis were no longer followed. Waste became a problem and with it flies spread and proliferated.

For 1,500 years during the Golden Age of Atlantis, animals and people were friends. They loved and honoured each other. There was no fear or danger: many animals were part of the family. Even when humans and animals started to eat flesh, this was always done by a divine contract. For example, the hungry person would telepathically contact the herd and the weakest member would offer itself as food. This sacrifice made him sacred and was part of the exchange between the two. This principle is still applied in the Native American Tribes, who took their wisdom from Atlantis. They will mentally ask an animal for permission before they hunt it.

In order to bring back the energy of pure Atlantis we must learn to honour animals and become friends with them once more.

EXERCISE: *Communicating with an Animal*

If you have a dog, cat or horse – even a mouse or rabbit – practise this exercise with them. If not, your neighbour may have a friendly domestic pet, sometimes birds will come to talk to you – and there are always horses and cows in the fields. The more of a rapport you already have with an animal, the easier it will be to connect. However, the most important thing is the love, empathy and good intention that you radiate in your aura.

It is easier to practise this exercise if your animal is in your physical presence, but if it is not, send an absent communication to it.

1. Sit quietly with your animal. Stroke it and whisper to it if you wish to, but this is not essential.
2. Imagine pink light coming from your heart centre and surrounding you. Then let it enfold the animal.
3. Mentally tell the animal that you love it and wish to communicate with it.
4. When you feel you have established a rapport, telepathically ask it a question.
5. Wait in a receptive mode for an answer to drop into your mind. This will usually come as a thought, which you may think is your own. The more you practise this, the more quickly you will be able to differentiate your own thoughts from the responses of the animal.
6. Sometimes the flash of response will drop in later – even the next day – so relax and enjoy this exercise without expectation or pressure.

CHAPTER 5

Homes and Leisure

Houses

In the golden times, the inhabitants of Atlantis, including the priests, were home-loving, family-orientated people. Their houses were simple: round or oblong and built in natural materials. Feng shui, or geomancy, was practised and so everything was curved or rounded, which was believed to be more harmonious to the human spirit and a better channel for the energy of the universe. Soft shapes also honoured the feminine principles of gentleness, caring and inclusiveness.

Each family had their own home, but work was communal. Of course, in the earliest days when everyone was single, each house was a basic one-room dwelling, for the immediate aim was to provide everyone with shelter. During the next phase, they considered longer-term needs. At this point, they started to build two-storey homes in which the living space was downstairs and the bedrooms were upstairs. The sleeping rooms were partitioned areas without doors. Some people reached the upper rooms by teleportation, though not everyone could do this. Most preferred to climb up, since there were always ladders, and people tended to do as much as they possibly could, physically, because they realised they were here to experience life in a body. Furthermore, it takes more energy to teleport than to walk up steps.

There were no bathrooms; everyone bathed together in open-air pools and saunas, in the warm climate. Nothing was wasted either. In the early years, communal toilets outside allowed human waste to be used for manure. Despite their amazing technological prowess and knowledge, life was simple, always ecological and natural.

DECORATION

Decoration was also simple, tending to be only a picture or mural on the downstairs walls created by artists for the householder. They painted animals, inspirational scenes from nature or abstract pictures in beautiful colours with a high spiritual energy. All things were designed to maintain the divine frequency.

Because colour affects us so profoundly, different ones were carefully chosen and applied. For example, red was used in work areas, while rooms used for creativity were orange, as were children's spaces. Appropriate colours were used for various age groups. For peace, and to raise the frequency, temples were painted in blue, mauve and green, while inspiration was induced with magenta. The only ornaments in the early days were from crystals that were programmed to light up in the evenings, or from glowing metals.

FURNISHINGS

Almost all furniture and utensils were handmade and carved with love so that they radiated high vibrations into the atmosphere. Because people loved making things, objects were rarely manifest from the ethers, even by those who had the power to do so freely. They found it much more satisfying to fashion their own creations. Every item radiates energy. That which is mass-produced, in an environment filled with fear or frustration, releases dark energy, which affects all who touch it. In Atlantis, at this time every single object was produced with love and considered to be sacred.

Beds were made of wooden boards, slightly elevated, with a soft cover, usually woven from cotton. The Atlanteans were intensely practical. They would never hurt an animal, but when it died naturally they would use the skins, and soft cushions to sit on were filled with chicken feathers or wool from sheep.

The homes all had fires inside them, needed less for warmth than for cooking. This nurturing role was usually undertaken by women, for they had chosen to incarnate in a female body to learn about and express their feminine energy. Currently, women still choose a female incarnation for the same reason. In those gentle times, however, women were treated as spiritual beings, whose homemaking skills were appreciated and valued. Furthermore, a woman's talents in all creative and artistic areas were honoured and encouraged. She was considered equal to a man, just different, and was definitely not a little woman at home. She also had certain powers, which made life easier. For instance, a woman could click her fingers and levitate a utensil into her hand from the other side of the room.

Outdoor Life

Most gardens also had a fire with which people would cook. Families and friends loved to sit out under the stars, round the open flames, and tell stories or sing together. They were very sociable people and a key to their contentment was frequent celebration. They honoured and gave thanks for birthdays, a good harvest, the full moon, special rains or anything that felt relevant. Naturally, they all ate together and blessed their food. They understood intuitively that blessed food is super charged with divine energy.

They did not need alcohol or drugs during the earlier period, for their happy spirits came from within. Mood-altering substances were sought only when the vibration of Atlantis started to fall.

Because nature and the outdoors were so important to them, Atlanteans appreciated their gardens, which were beautiful and natural. They loved wild flowers, but did not cultivate them. Nor were their lawns manicured in the early days, although they were kept in check and grazed by sheep or goats. Their surroundings were enriched with beautifully-carved pieces of wood or special stones. Moving water played an important role in their well-being and many had pools and fountains in their homes or gardens. They would spend time by them, meditating and simply being, relaxing to the sound and movement of water. Later, in the towns, swimming pools were plentiful. Temples also had running water or fountains in their central areas of worship.

Atlanteans knew that everything, including stones, crystals, trees, plants and animals, is a materialisation of divine life force. All is God. Therefore, they honoured and accepted every single thing as having an important role in their lives. Because these simple people recognised the Divine in all things, crystals, plants and creatures responded to them and worked with them. For example, they could communicate with the elemental life force within a tree and ask it to grow into a shape that would shade or shelter them.

In the Aquarian Age we are trying to get back to being God. The Atlanteans knew they were God.

The Atlanteans kept their frequency high by relaxing, enjoying their leisure and being sociable. They were light, fun-filled, happy people. Families lived together and, as more generations came in, they would extend their homes or at least live in the same area. They loved the company of others because they exchanged energy, so they invited other family groups to their homes to share simple food. They enlivened these meetings with music, storytelling, acting and dancing, all of which were popular pastimes at gatherings. Because their right brains were developed and their memory banks expanded, they had enormous capacity to remember stories in intricate detail.

Their pleasures were innocent. They picked berries together as a family, and enjoyed walking alone or with others in nature and picnicking by rivers. They all swam like fish and especially loved to swim with their friends, the dolphins, in the sea or in huge pools that they had constructed for them. Or they would make rafts, or rig up sails on a boat to catch the wind. They also played games together: football, catch or rounders, with the emphasis on simple fun.

Society and Culture

Atlanteans loved their homes and families as well as their animals, which were always part of the household and considered to be important family members.

Women would sit outside in a cluster, creating pottery, weaving or sewing together. Clothing was simple, they used wool, cotton and silk, dyeing the cloth with natural plant or shell dyes. People were dressed in tunics, which were often purple, dyed with the plentiful murex seashells. Their only decoration would be a crystal attuned to higher consciousness.

The early settlers soon started to make music. They began with wind instruments, like flutes and lutes, made from reeds and animal bones. Nothing was ever assumed or taken for granted, so they would ask an animal for permission to use its bones before it died. Of course, all animals died of natural causes in these early days.

Drums, cymbals and bells were very popular from the first. Soon people fashioned metal tubes of different lengths and fastened them together to look like several panpipes in a row. They would hit the individual pipes with a stick covered in something soft and this created beautiful notes. The metals came from another planet, so we cannot recreate these instruments or sounds nowadays. Atlanteans also made melodies with hanging crystals. Lastly, they developed the skills to make stringed instruments and to fashion huge harps.

The people loved to sing or chant together and to listen to music, to allow the vibrations to flow through their bodies. One composition might enable a person to experience power; another, sensual, calming notes. A concert would be dedicated to specific music, for instance sacred chanting or uplifting chords. They built vast sound chambers with extraordinary acoustics where concerts could be performed and people gathered for the social event as well as the opportunity to be inspired. They also created sound chambers within temples for healing.

All levels and tastes of music were catered for, but there was no heavy metal. Children were not off balance then as they are now, so there was no call for it. It was only in later Atlantis, as the frequency became discordant and people needed to express their disharmony, that rock-type music became popular.

Creativity and art was valued and encouraged. Art exhibitions were very popular, as artists wanted to spread the energy of their creations for people to experience. Shapes, colours and compositions within a painting radiate specific vibrations and the painters of early Atlantis wished to express the glory of creation. In due course, huge exhibition halls were built with several floors; each floor dedicated to a particular frequency. All the paintings, sculptures, music and lighting on a particular floor would resonate to the same pulse. The people who desired that tone would come to bathe in it. They also met their friends at the exhibitions as the social aspects of the events were valued.

The people loved to keep their physical bodies fit and in due course challenged each other to races. This was always done for fun and to extend themselves; competition was never undertaken from ego, but was a medium for developing excellence. Eventually, one town would invite another to a match and each centre would take turns to host these, which were the forerunner of the Olympic games as we know them today. It was a time of celebration and friendship, and an opportunity to expand physical boundaries. Horses raced each other too. They ran without riders, not because they were trained to, but because they wanted to.

Atlanteans learnt that simplicity was one of the keys to keeping their energy pure. Their daily life was spent in a combination of work, social and family life, contemplation, leisure and thanksgiving.

EXERCISE: *Expressing Your Creativity*

1. Decide on a quality that you would like to express. It might be tranquillity, joy, aspiration or anything else you might choose.
2. Find a medium with which you would like to create. It could be paint or crayons, sand, clay, wood, music or something completely different.
3. Sit in quiet contemplation for a few moments. Feel the quality inside you and focus on it.
   - What colour is it?
   - What sound it is?
   - How does it feel? Is it thick, thin, silky, rough or sensuous?
   - Does it express an element? Water, fire, air, earth, ethers?
   - How does it smell and taste?
   - What shape does it have?
   - What does it look like?
4. Now express it with your medium. This does not have to be a work of genius. No one else need see it. It is simply an expression of a divine aspect of yourself. The more often you do this exercise, the more deeply you will absorb the quality and be able to express it in your life.

EXERCISE: *Celebrating*

Every day is a celebration. What can you celebrate today? How are you going to do it? Celebrate your health by lighting a candle and giving thanks, celebrate the beauty of the flowers by saying a few words of thanks, celebrate a beautiful sunset by opening your arms in a gesture of expansion.

CHAPTER 6

Farming

Up to the decline of Atlantis, everyone was vegetarian, although they accepted the animals' offerings, such as wool, milk, feathers or eggs. They believed that the eating of flesh would lower their frequency and shut down their psychic abilities, so their food was derived from plants, nuts, seeds, berries, eggs and dairy produce. At the beginning all plants were eaten raw, but quite quickly in the evolution of the community they began to cook them lightly.

Working with Nature

Because their spiritual lives were aligned to the natural world, people respected and honoured the rhythms and needs of nature. So the farmers planted and harvested appropriately for each type of plant, according to the phases of the moon. The Atlanteans also ate in tune with the seasons. They realised that the human body is in harmony with all of nature, so correct food was available at the perfect timing for the body's needs. The same applied to location. The food growing in the North Islands was exactly attuned to the requirements of the people living there, as was that on the South Islands. These principles are still divinely correct at the current time. Local food in season is imbued with perfect nutrients for the people living in that place. In the Golden Age this was understood, and the concept of transporting God-given food somewhere else was inconceivable. Scientists have now discovered that the amino acids in soya differ according to the latitude at which they are grown and correspond to the nutritional needs of animals and humans in each area.

The farmers placed companion plants together for their mutual support and protection, and watched and listened to their plants, telepathically receiving information from them. The mighty Thoth, later known as Hermes Trismegistus, taught the early settlers that there is a harmony and correspondence in every living thing in the universe, including the movement of planets, tides and currents, animals, humans, plants, crystals – everything. All the cosmos responds to certain harmonies and combinations of notes, which are tuned to the same scale. This means that appropriate tunes and rhythms, synchronised to the cellular structure of a human, will heal that person. The correct notes will also help plants to grow healthy and abundant. Atlanteans learnt that plants respond to certain types of music and so they sang and chanted to them, using a harmonious, loving vibration to encourage their yield. It was also considered perfectly natural to sit amongst their vegetables and talk to them. This, of course, allowed a flow of prana or life force to be exchanged between humans and nature. We discuss sound healing in more detail later.

Now, when someone has a special empathy with flowers, which grow abundantly for him, we say he has green fingers. These people inevitably talk aloud or silently to their plants. Love is a cosmic force, which affects humans, plants, rocks and Gaia herself. In modern times many experiments have been undertaken that have shown that plants shrivel and die when bombarded with fractured rock music. In contrast, they grow lush and prolific when played classical music, especially baroque music or sacred Indian music.

CRYSTALS FOR PLANTS

Around the plants, the Atlanteans placed crystals that automatically vibrated with them, which helped them to grow and kept them healthy. Other plants that were superabundant and tended to take over were surrounded by specifically-programmed quartz crystals to persuade them to remain contained. Dendritic agate enhanced the yield of crops and was used to maintain the health of house plants. It also stabilised the vortices within the Earth's energy field.

Boji stones are formed of dense sand, with an outer layer containing iron particles and sand so tightly compacted that they feel like iron to the touch. The particular vibration they emanate is beneficial to crops and plants and so these stones were arranged amongst the foliage. There are two types of boji stones, one smooth, which carries feminine energy, and the other with protrusions, which holds the masculine energy. They were used in perfect balance.

Lithium quartz was plentiful and frequently used to heal plants and animals. It also purifies water. Of course this was not necessary in the Golden Age, but later this crystal was placed in pools and drinking water. It is helpful in current times to place a lithium quartz in a jug or glass of bottled, tap or filtered water for purification. If the water is put into a blue glass and placed in sunlight, this can charge up the water with divine energy. Remember, if you pour some of this sacred liquid into a local river or pool, it will act homoeopathically, thus helping to purify and raise the vibration of the larger body of water.

Green tourmaline was popular because it has the power to heal all plants and maintain the energy of the garden. This was partly because it has a strong connection with the devas, the nature spirits that look after trees, plants, rivers, mountains and all aspects of nature. The farmers were very aware of the elves, fairies, gnomes, salamanders, undines and other nature spirits, and would co-operate with them.

As a result of working in harmony with nature, the farmers produced food that was rich in nourishment in a way that is beyond our comprehension now. It contained prana, divine life force, so that very little food was needed.

CULTIVATION

Plants and vegetables were tended by specialist farmers, though the whole community automatically helped with harvesting. Everything was placed in storage, where families helped themselves freely to whatever they needed. Their diet was partly corn-based, but they grew potatoes and all sorts of vegetables, nuts and fruits.

Even in the earliest days the Atlanteans used a form of hydroponics, which ensured that the plants had the right amount of moisture and light. They created covered stands, at waist level, in which to grow their seedlings, providing perfect conditions. These looked similar to our current glasshouses, but they were made of neither polythene nor glass. Instead they used a highly effective material, which we no longer have the technology to produce.

The five islands of Atlantis that made up Golden Atlantis were spread over a considerable area. There was a huge distance from north to south, which meant there were climate differences. In the north they cultivated grapes, blueberries, boysenberries, cherries and nuts, but it was too warm for apples. Further south they grew oranges, lemons, limes, grapefruit and figs, while in the most southern island, mangoes, pineapples, coconuts, papayas and pomegranates were prolific. Atlanteans loved to make a variety of fruit drinks, especially from pomegranates.

Other specialists, who loved animals, cared for the cattle, sheep and other creatures. These farmers all worked together within the communities, supporting each other and enjoying their roles. They honoured the animals and valued the food they offered. They would never assume the right to take milk or wool, but would always ask the animal for it and be grateful when it was given. Dedicated beekeepers cared for the bees and created simple hives, asking permission to take the honey offered.

Trees

Trees are the lungs of the planet, which balance the atmosphere. They are very benevolent and spread love. People sense this, which is why, even in our cynical times, people love to sit under trees or walk in the woods. Trees also have a role as keepers of ancient wisdom, for they store the history and the wisdom of the land. A tree could tell you what has happened to the soil around it since time began. If there is pollution, an infestation of insects or weather changes, they will hold the information. The trees of Atlantis also held the data on the experiment so that the Intergalactic Council could use the information encoded within them to understand what went wrong and learn from it.

A variety of timber grew on the different islands. There were no oak, ash, elm, beech, chestnut, larch, or sycamore trees, which grow in current northern climes. But palms, eucalyptuses, maples, willows, poplars, olives, pines, sandalwoods, cypresses, and some others that are now extinct, abounded. The Atlanteans particularly loved trees. They would sit and lean against their trunks to restore their equilibrium and energy. And they danced around them at their ceremonies.

In the golden times, the soil was rich and fertile. The weather was clement and rainfall was perfect, controlled by the energy biodome that covered Atlantis. Plants, grown in tune with universal energies, were full of flavour and goodness. Consequently people had to expend very little time or energy to meet their basic nourishment needs. Furthermore, they had no material desires to amass goods or to prove themselves better than another, so they spent their time in creative pursuits: drawing, painting, sculpting or fashioning items of beauty. They loved to play music or relax in nature and have fun with their family, friends and animals.

It is when we become busy and spend too much time thinking

that we disconnect from our true selves. The early Atlanteans lived peaceful, contemplative, harmonious lives, which kept their connections to the spiritual world pure and their right brains open. They also spent all day outside, in nature – at one with All That Is since nature and the Divine are connected.

Plants, like people, respond to positive and negative emotions and vibrations, whether it be through music, thought or being spoken to harshly or lovingly. Try the following exercise and see for yourself what happens.

EXERCISE: *Using the Power of Love and Hate*
1. Take two identical pots and plant seeds in each one, in similar soil.
2. Write 'love', 'peace' and 'thanks' on a piece of paper, and attach this to one pot.
3. Write 'hate', 'no good', 'horrible' on another piece of paper and attach it to the second pot.
4. Water each pot in the same way. As you do so, tell the seeds in the first pot that you love them, that they are doing well. Visualise them growing abundantly and tell them how pleased you are with them. Explain that you are proud of them. But tell the seeds in the second pot that they are no good, that you hate them, and that they are miserable, horrible plants and don't deserve to do well.
5. Watch the results.

CHAPTER 7

Life After the Second Generation

A Harmonious Community

For hundreds of years the Atlanteans maintained heaven on Earth. Sharing, caring, personal development and responsibility were qualities that were nurtured and honoured, so the communities were thriving, happy places.

The High Priest or Priestess who ruled the tribe spent some of their time in the Temple of Poseidon and some in the community, where they were available for the inhabitants to consult. They were revered and loved as people of the highest integrity and honour. Every decision they made was for the highest good of the citizens, who knew this and respected their decisions. Furthermore, because the leaders were just, everyone accepted that the system was fair. It meant that there was a high level of trust between the governors and what would now be called their constituents. Because of this the people also devoted everything to the community. Nothing was sought for personal gain.

Until the decline, there was no money, as no one needed it. Produce of every description: food, cloth, furniture, paintings or tools were placed in a central complex and people helped themselves to whatever they needed. As there was plenty for all, no one ever took more than their immediate requirements. Why should they? Open hearts do not fear lack, they embrace abundance. And, responding to the spiritual law of balance, people always gave back in some way for anything they received. Because everyone felt happy and valued, they gave freely and a sense of satisfaction was their reward. Feeling fulfilled, they had no room for envy or jealousy. When the whole community is co-operating towards a vision greater than themselves, no one cheats or betrays. There was no rapacious tax system and therefore no place for creative accountancy. Every single individual joyfully supported and generously contributed to the whole.

The atmosphere everywhere was peaceful. There was no sound of traffic, power tools, loud discordant music or even raucous voices. Everyone was attuned to nature and the quiet and stillness of Gaia, so all were consequently serene and contented. They had plenty of leisure time, always felt loved and included, served the community by doing what they most wanted to do and were healthy. It was a time of laughter and happiness.

Rites of Passage for Women

In early Atlantis, as they still do, women went through a series of inner initiations. The first was the onset of menstruation, which was greeted and celebrated as the girl's introduction to womanhood. Their menses became a source of pride and honour. The second, and deeper, initiation was that of childbirth, which was painful but not excessively so. When the baby was born, the people were awed to see that the mother's aura became a beautiful light green-blue, which enfolded, nurtured and protected the newborn. This colour remained in the mother's aura for two years after the birth. During that time, if she was to be away from the child, she would visualise her infant being surrounded in this aquamarine colour, so that it felt the safety of its mother. Now, when a mother gives birth, Mother Mary and her angels surround her and the baby in deeper blue. This stronger colour is needed because we live at a lower frequency and a more protective shade is required. As during Atlantean times, the mother's aura contains this radiant blue for two years. If a child is to be left with someone else, it is important to surround it in the Mary blue, so that it feels safe and secure. To do this, visualise the child with the beautiful blue surrounding it. The third initiation was when the blood stopped flowing and a woman became a Wise One, revered for the knowledge and experience she could offer.

Rites of Passage for Men

Male initiation to manhood took place at the age of thirteen, when the boy left his family and underwent special teachings as well as tests of physical endurance. He returned to the community as a man who was proud of and confident in his manhood. He was ready to use his superior physical strength to look after and protect the young and weak and to provide an example to growing boys.

Celebration

The people of this time were social and gregarious and they loved to celebrate. Communities who rejoice together tend to be happy ones. Thanksgiving parties and ceremonies bond people in a common cause.

These people did not use drugs or any mood or mind-altering substances. They had no need, for there were no stresses to battle, discontent to bury or inner demons to escape. They were aware that the product of certain plants, like cannabis, tobacco or coffee, clouds the aura, blurring psychic perceptions and they had no desire to do that.

LSD is an artificially produced chemical that changes the pattern of brainwaves so that the user becomes mentally out of synch and can never get into synch again. This destroys the possibility of spiritual connection for that lifetime. Drugs with a similar effect were produced when the power and purity of Atlantis started to decline. At that time the inhabitants' psychic powers waned and they often took such chemicals to open themselves up to becoming psychic again.

This is happening again in current times, where youngsters are turning en masse to drugs of all kinds for relief from life and to access other-worldly experiences. But this creates a false experience, which is not based on a solid spiritual foundation. What these drug takers see in the inner planes is often illusion and projection, but because they picture it so clearly they believe it to be the objective truth. In pure Atlantis all celebrations were highly spiritual, drug-free times of gratitude.

In current times, some people feel a real drive to make a connection with the Divine. Shaaron has discovered through the soul readings she does that people will even subconsciously abuse alcohol, narcotics and other mood-altering substances as a means of getting into an AA twelve step programme. This programme is all about surrendering to a higher power, particularly steps 3 and 11, which are:

Step 3. I make a decision to turn my will and my life over to the care of God, as I understand him.

Step 11. I seek through prayer and meditation to improve my conscious contact with God, as I understand Him, praying only for knowledge of His will for me and the power to carry that out.

The twelve steps are excellent as a stepping-stone to self-responsibility. This often marks the beginning of a person's spiritual journey, leading to the ascension pathway.

Right Brain/Left Brain

In the halcyon days of Atlantis, the people were predominantly right-brain dominant, and like all right-brain societies they were inclusive, so everyone was cared for and treated with compassion. Love, generosity, sharing and caring were valued qualities, as were creativity and artistic expression. The people were relaxed, contemplative and inclined to mysticism. Their original and creative minds enabled them to develop spiritual technology, which was awesome in its application, but was always harmless to humans, animals and nature, which they revered and honoured.

All cultures that have a vision beyond the self, such as the Aborigines, Native American Indians or Kahunas, are continuous, unlike later Atlantis and modern left-brain societies, where cliques, hierarchies and fractured governments, motivated by ego, predominate. Where people are striving, busy and stressed, emotions are denied or derided. The head and heart then separate, and this allows people and governments to act with great cruelty, resulting in violence, abuse and war. Today, in striving discontent, we move the world forward with science and technology, but rape the Earth of minerals and oil and are careless of pollution. Where there is no reverence for nature, there is a feeling of separation from it, which makes people feel they have the right to change it, genetically modify it, clone it or damage it by chopping down its forests and polluting its rivers. Disconnection from the heart, and its consequences of cruelty, slavery and injustice, also took place when Atlantis devolved, but even in their most dire times they rejected the idea of using fossil fuel because of the damage it would cause to the plant. However, in the darkest days they did clone, genetically modify, and implant people and plants.

Right-brain societies are inevitably child centred, for children are considered to be a gift to the community. In Atlantis, the little ones were loved, honoured and included, even in elementary decision making. It was considered to be a collective responsibility to pass on the traditions and wisdom to the next generation, for they had no individual wealth to leave as a legacy.

EXERCISE: *Right- or Left-Brain Dominant?*

Take the following quick and easy test to see if you are left- or right-brain dominant. Cover the answers until you are ready to check your balance. Read the statements below and every time one resonates with you, place a tick next to it, using the grid provided. When you have done that go to the answers at the end of the chapter and for every tick box in the grid, note whether the statement is an L or an R, and write it in the column to the right. Count up the number of L's and R's; whichever has the higher amount represents your dominance. If the numbers are close, it means you use both sides of your brain equally.

Statement	*Tick* (if appropriate)	*L/R*
1. I am neat and tidy		
2. I keep a diary		
3. I often daydream		
4. I like to wander in nature		
5. My guesses are often right		
6. I would make a good editor		
7. I gesture with my hands when I talk		
8. I tackle problems logically		
9. I work hard for what I want		
10. I am intuitive		
11. I consider myself a down-to-earth person		
12. I have a vision for the world		

Statement	Tick (if appropriate)	L/R
13. I express myself well with words		
14. I wanted to be an artist, designer or musician		
15. I enjoy fantasy stories		
16. I am good at mathematics		
17. I am goal-orientated		
18. I love to dance		
19. I like to be practical		
20. I always follow my hunches		
21. I can't relate to psychic things		
22. I get bored with routine		
23. When people ask a question, I turn my head to the left		
24. I always take a familiar route		
25. I enjoy learning facts		
26. I wanted to be a solicitor, accountant or dentist		
27. I like to know the facts before I make a decision		
28. Sometimes I lose time		
29. I love the full moon		

Statement	Tick (if appropriate)	L/R
30. I like routine		
31. I love music		
32. When asked a question, I turn my head to the right		
33. I write lists		
34. I have an active imagination		
35. Sometimes I just know the answer		
36. I like co-operating with others		
37. I prefer to read a book than watch the film made from it		
38. I like to be in charge		
39. I like to see the whole picture		
40. I sense atmospheres in a room		

Answers to the exercise

1. L	9. L	17. L	25. L	33. L
2. L	10. R	18. R	26. L	34. R
3. R	11. L	19. L	27. L	35. R
4. R	12. R	20. R	28. R	36. R
5. R	13. L	21. L	29. R	37. L
6. L	14. R	22. R	30. L	38. L
7. R	15. R	23. R	31. R	39. R
8. L	16. L	24. L	32. L	40. R

A left-brain person would be logical, rational, cerebral, practical, hierarchical, punctual, a lover of routine, and would like order and discipline. They would have an eye for detail. The downside of this is that they are split between the head and heart, which can result in a lack of feeling for other people. They would also tend to be cynical as they have disconnected from spirit.

Right-brain people are inclusive, empathetic, visionary, unbounded, artistic, creative, imaginative, spiritual, flowing and psychic. The downside is that because they lack focus, they frequently have difficulty in accomplishing things and consequently make slower progress. They can also be fearful and superstitious.

The aim for the new age is to balance the right- and left-brain qualities.

CHAPTER 8

Evolution of Society

Development of Education

As the population increased, priests trained in specialist functions, one of which was education. Temples, or parts of them, were dedicated to this. Just as they did when the first children arrived, the teacher priests taught the children telepathically. They imparted spiritual information and cosmic truths while the little ones were relaxed and open to higher knowledge. In addition, each individual had his or her own teaching crystal.

Crystals have a consciousness. They are in touch with each other and transfer energy. Quartz can transfer information directly to quartz and two amethysts communicate clearly, but an amethyst and a rose quartz would communicate less clearly. It is a matter of compatibility. Just as we resonate with certain people, crystals automatically resonate with other crystals that do a similar type of work.

When the main teaching priest in the Temple of Poseidon planned a lesson, he programmed a crystal with the information he wanted to impart to certain children or adults. Once the lesson was programmed into the crystal, five, twenty or even more crystals would be placed round it, ready to receive the information. They could be left together for minutes or even hours for the transfer to take place. When this was done the main teaching priest would teleport them to the appropriate school. If several children needed the same lesson, the file was sent to all of them. Children were taught to place the quartz teaching crystal on their third eye and download the information they needed. Boys and girls were considered equal, but different and received education according to their individual aptitude.

The teaching temples were designed to enable a pupil to relax deeply. It was considered futile to teach a child who had any level of stress, as this inhibits the capacity to learn. So a 'school' was a welcoming, friendly place, where calming music was played, enhanced with soothing aromas and soft lighting. Even at advanced levels it was recognised that a student learnt more easily if the lessons were enjoyable. Appropriate coloured lights were used according to the child's age and level of receptivity, since colour is important in assisting the learning process.

Our internet system reflects how the Atlanteans worked. The Great Crystal had all knowledge, but instead of downloading the information they wanted onto their laptop or desktop via a keyboard, they could obtain the information they were allowed to access by concentrating on the crystal. They would ask their questions and receive the information directly into their third eye.

Then, just as now, not all information was available to everyone. Today you need a password to get onto a restricted site as we use codes to limit access. In Atlantis, the priests would be able to block and redirect information by using the power of their thoughts.

Technology

When the Intergalactic Council believed that the populace was ready for another level of technology, they would programme the Great Crystal with new technological information. They did this in exactly the same way that we programme computers today, but they used telepathy rather than a keyboard. Within the main temple in each of the twelve communities there was also a large quartz crystal with the qualities of a computer. The information was downloaded from the 'mainframe' – the Great Crystal in the Temple of Poseidon – to the individual temple crystals. The Mage, the highly evolved shaman attached to each centre, would go into deep trance and draw the information from the crystal. When he had received and understood it, he would pass it on to the people. For example, when the Intergalactic Council decided it was time to build roads to replace the stony tracks, this vision, together with the technology to create the streets, was passed down through a teaching crystal.

The local people planned where the roads were needed and would visualise them. This was their contribution to the project and enabled everyone to feel they had taken part in a joint venture. The Mage, supported by his community, would send forth streams of energy, which created a smooth, flat material, which surfaced the road. The constituents of this material are no longer present on our planet. It looked something like sophisticated tarmac, but was utterly different.

Travel

At the very beginning, people walked along the paths they had worn between locations, but soon they developed carts and asked the horses to help pull them. The horses were aware that this was part of their service contract and were happy to oblige. In accordance with their rustic lifestyle, this is how they moved bags of corn from one place to another.

It was not long before the technology of road building was passed down to them, which made journeys easier for the general population. The priests, and those of the population whose skills were sufficiently advanced, used teleportation and telekinesis to transport goods.

Soon, using their spiritual powers, they developed other methods of travel. At the age of seven, during a ceremony in the local Temple of Sound, which we explain more fully later, each child was presented with a metal plate or tray tuned to the vibration of his name, so that he could travel above the ley lines – the energy lines around the planet.

The owner of the plate sat on the tray and hit it with a special stick or wand, which created a specific vibration so that it would rise above the ground. By focusing on his desired destination, the traveller could direct his tray accordingly. Many adults travelled locally by the same method. We believe that the universal myth of the magic carpet came from stories passed down about these plates.

The metals of each tray were chosen according to the planet of the person's origin and most of these are no longer present on the Earth. The universe works on a 'need to have' basis. As something is necessary, it becomes available, and when our frequency rises again we will once more be able to access the cosmic materials that have currently been withdrawn.

Because of the magnetic force of the ley lines, when powered by the sun or moon, it was much easier to travel along them in daylight or at full moon – and impossible when there was an eclipse. Accordingly the Magi kept advanced calendars, which notified everyone of the lunar phases, and predicted solar or lunar eclipses. It was vitally important to know when there was no power, for at those times all flying craft had to land.

Of course, the most powerful time for travel was at the full moon, which was a period of great female potency because this was when women collectively menstruated. (This still happens in indigenous cultures which work with the natural cycles of life, or where groups of women, such as nuns, live together). On that night each month, certain gifted women flew along the ley lines to meet together, to talk, share their secrets and expand their sacred knowledge.

In early Atlantis, at a time when female wisdom was admired and revered, this practice was accepted as normal. However, as Atlantis devolved, the superior female wisdom and power was considered to be a threat by the men, who did not work together as the women did. The physically stronger males started to make women subservient, even forcing them to cover their heads and wear rings as a symbol of inferiority and ownership.

Centuries later, in the dark days of the Middle Ages, when the masculine-dominated church attempted to destroy the feminine power, wise women, mediums, healers and herbalists were burnt at the stake. In order to frighten people into acceptance, wise women were depicted as black witches flying across the full moon. This was a distortion of a memory, lingering in human consciousness, from Atlantis.

Atlantean families tended to stay together and extended their homes to accommodate new generations. At the same time, bloodlines were discouraged from intermarrying. So there were many inter-community functions, sporting events, creative exhibitions, concerts and celebrations to which the people from the other tribes were invited and which allowed young people to meet and marry. The bride or bridegroom would join the partner's family, so inevitably there was much travelling to visit and keep in touch.

Many people travelled on huge airbuses, which moved along the various frequencies at differing heights. They gathered at stations to get onto their transports, which travelled at what would now be inconceivably high speeds, silently and without causing any pollution.

Mental Healing

As society expanded, there were accidents or healing challenges when an individual's chakras became unbalanced. Sick people were taken to healing temples where skilled healer priests would use crystal laser wands to perform surgery, create specific notes and tones to knit bones, or shine colour to rebalance people.

If the imbalance was mental and the person's behaviour became antisocial, he was taken to a healing temple. Because everyone was vibrating at a fifth-dimensional frequency and was aware of spiritual law, the individual always wanted to realign to his true soul energy. First, he received counselling from the priests, who looked for the source of the problem. The offender then freely gave permission to allow himself to be hypnotised by magnetism, which forced his spirit out of his body. At this point, a Mage examined him and marked his body to indicate where the physical manifestation of disorder was located. Healers beamed energy into these specific points, to atrophy the blood vessels serving relevant organs or to flood the cells with blood, as necessary.

While this was taking place, a trained priest communicated telepathically with the person's spirit, raising his consciousness to align with his true soul vibration. The modern equivalent is hypnotherapy, in which a patient's emotional, mental and spiritual problems can be addressed and reprogrammed, while he or she is in trance. Even though our understanding is not nearly as advanced as it was in Atlantis, applied by a skilled practitioner, this form of therapy can be extremely helpful and effective.

At this time of Atlantis, there was no need for prisons and when treated at the healing temples no one ever reoffended.

EXERCISE: *Full Moon Closure*
Because full moon is a time of completion, it powerfully assists with healing, releasing and sealing that which no longer serves you. Many people move into the new without closing the old. For example, when you left home, did you embrace your future without having a ceremony of closure for the past? Or have you ever started a different job without shutting the doors to the former one? Or have you left a relationship without fully saying

goodbye? We no longer tend to celebrate endings, but this is vitally important because it leaves energetic fragments in your aura when you do not.

In the few days leading up to the full moon, list any areas of your life in which you wish to exercise closure. Then, on the night of the full moon, undertake the following meditation, which should be done outside if possible. If this is not practical, do not be too concerned – the moon's energy will still assist your intention.

1. Light a candle and an oil burner or incense.
2. Play soft music, and if you have a piece of moonstone wear it or place it beside you.
3. The colour of completion is gold, so place your candle on a piece of gold silk.
4. Close your eyes and allow the moonlight to shine onto your face or, if you are inside, imagine it and feel it.
5. Visualise the first scenario that you wish to close. As you review this scene, consciously say 'Goodbye'. Then thank the people and situation for the experience, which has enabled you to become the person you are today.
6. Feel yourself releasing every aspect of the old emotional, mental, physical and personal and see it disappear.
7. Repeat this for any other closures you wish to make.
8. Sit quietly for a few minutes, feeling the moonlight clearing you.
9. Open your eyes. Breathe deeply and have a drink of water.

CHAPTER 9

Spirituality

Ceremonies at Stone Circles

The people loved to take part in rituals and ceremonies, and these sacred celebrations held the communities together. They knew that genuine gratitude from the heart is one of the most powerful of energies which literally moves the universe in response, so all spiritual devotion was based on thanksgiving. They focused on sending out a stream of thanks and continuously counted their blessings. Each time anyone does this, of course, their aura lights up and they draw more good things to them. The early Atlanteans radiated light.

Because the weather was controlled by the Alta and was clement, the communities were able to meet outside in the beauty of natural surroundings, where they built stone circles. Each stone was carefully chosen for its shape and qualities. Some of them were levitated from a distance by telekinesis, sound and crystal power, and then they were very carefully put in place. The stones were often concave, with the effect that the circle became a sound chamber where the priests would tone and chant.

Whenever there was a gathering, the participants would walk to the stone circles along a ley line, which enabled them to absorb the special magnetic energy through their feet. This raised their vibration and brought them into divine alignment for the ritual. Then they would wind up the frequency of the circle by walking round the stones, singing and chanting as they did so. The priests would enter the ring, give thanks, and made invocations by chanting special sounds or notes. When they finished they unwound the energy by pacing anti-clockwise, exactly as you would walk a sacred labyrinth.

They also angled the stone circles towards one of the star systems, for example, Orion, so that the wisdom from the Masters of Orion could be drawn down to them as they performed their rites. Or they might direct the stones towards the Pleiades to bring in healing energy, or towards Sirius to bring in spiritual technology. They were then bathed in high-frequency light from that star system, which they could absorb into their consciousness.

The stone circles were built above the point where underground streams crossed, so the power of the ceremony and the wisdom of the extraterrestrials passed through the ring of people into the water and was carried round Atlantis through the system of waterways. This meant that the water was not only clear and pure, it was also constantly blessed and filled with a high-frequency energy, so that when people drank it, swam or bathed in it, they received continuous blessings.

In our current times, the food we eat is often lifeless and the water of suspect quality. In addition, most people no longer bless food and drink. Blessing it awakens the spiritual life force within it. Both Kirlian and aura photographs taken of a meal before and after it is blessed show an amazing difference. The divine shower of light that is invoked literally brings the food to life.

The same applies to water. The human body is ninety per cent water, and it is essential for our health and well-being. When it is polluted and contaminated, our frequency is dramatically lowered. In the amazing book *The Hidden Messages in Water*, by Masaru Emoto, the author displays photographs of crystals of water. From tap water in cities throughout the world, the crystals are ghastly dark, deformed and grotesque. From water that is pure and clear, they are stunningly beautiful. Some of the most glorious crystals were from water that had been prayed over or filled with thoughts of love or gratitude. He demonstrates that even writing the words 'thank you' or 'love' on a piece of paper and sticking it onto a jug full of water can affect the crystals in the liquid. Each time we stand by a lake, stream, river or the sea, we have the power to change its quality with our love, gratitude and prayers.

After the ceremonies in those halcyon days of Golden Atlantis, filled with light and joy, families and communities would cluster round the stones in groups and relate tales, sing and chant. Children were encouraged to tell stories so that they practised fully using their memory banks. The people experienced deep peace and belonging. Drawn to the energy of the rituals, animals would join the humans and bathe in the glorious light with them.

Spiritual Labyrinth

Then, as now, a labyrinth was a powerful and symbolic shape. As you walk into and out of one that is marked on the ground, or trace it with your finger, you are symbolically travelling the sacred journey of your life: going into the heart of your being, then returning out into the world again. The labyrinth itself has a cross in its centre, surrounded by a spiral. Many people think that it is the same as a maze. However, a maze is a puzzle, which engages the left brain to solve, whereas the labyrinth is a right-brain meditative journey, which opens you up spiritually.

Labyrinth

TO DRAW A LABYRINTH

In order to draw your own labyrinth, follow the instructions below in conjunction with the series of illustrations.

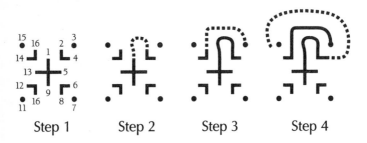

| Step 1 | Step 2 | Step 3 | Step 4 |

Step 1. Draw the initial grid, as illustrated above.

Step 2. Draw a line from position 2 to 1.

Step 3. Draw a line from position 3 to 16.

Step 4. Draw a line from position 4 to 15. Now continue drawing lines, as follows:

Step 5. From 5 to 14.

Step 6. From 6 to 13.

Step 7. From 7 to 12.

Step 8. From 8 to 11.

Step 9. From 9 to 10.

Passing Over

Atlanteans understood the principles of reincarnation. They knew that their spirit would go on an onward journey when their body died and would return 'home' for a period of readjustment and learning. Their spirit might very well receive training in other galaxies or star systems and then come back to Earth to learn more or to help others.

There was no waste or pollution in pure Atlantis. The bodies were neither cremated nor buried. Instead they were transported to special chambers in which particular vibrations were used that returned the physical body to its energy form. The family would dress the body ready for onward transmission, and take it to the huge room where it was placed into a vast coffin-like chamber. This ceremony was considered to be of profound importance and was performed by the Magi.

When someone died, everyone brought flowers since the pure energy could act as a booster rocket to help the spirit of the deceased on its way. In the early times of Atlantis, many of the people could consciously choose when they wanted to leave Earth and they would make controlled exists. In current times, high-vibration people can still do this: for instance, it is recorded that the revered guru Yogananda told his devotees when he would leave his body.

Part of the experience of life on Earth was to experience and deal with emotions so, despite their high level of spiritual awareness, the people still mourned and felt a great sense of loss at the departure of their loved ones. This was understood and they were encouraged to express their feelings so that the emotional energy would be released. They soon learnt that when emotions are denied, they remain like heavy clouds in our energy fields and cause our health to deteriorate.

Angels and Unicorns

Because the energy of the Atlanteans was so pure, only the purest and most beautiful angels of light acted as guardians. The light of guardian angels was similar to the frequency of archangels now. There were also many other angels present to help people, all of a very high vibration. Because of their high vibration, the people could see, sense and communicate telepathically with the angels. Just as now, angels held the divine blueprint of each person and whispered encouragement to each of them. Because everyone was so much more receptive, this was accepted as natural and normal.

In the same way that everyone had an angel to guide and assist his journey, each person also had a unicorn. These beautiful ethereal white horses have pure light, in the shape of a spiralling horn, pouring from their third eyes – visible radiations of spiritual energy. This energy is the same as an angel's wings. Unicorns came from Lakuma, the ascended star near Sirius, which is the spiritual home of all horses, and in the golden days they held the frequency of purity and divine innocence steady on Earth. They were also keepers of myth and magic. They radiated dignity, self-worth, honour, beauty, grace, healing, joy, peace, transmutation and clarity, so people were unconsciously influenced by these great qualities.

When Atlantis started to devolve, the settlers could no longer access the unicorns and highly-evolved angels of light, nor could their pure essences remain in the low vibrations, so they withdrew. Now that Earth is starting to evolve once more, angels – and even archangels – have been flocking to help us. In recent times, unicorns have started to return to help with this process. The concentration of the entire universe is on Earth. They all want our planet to ascend.

EXERCISE: *Thank-you Walk*
Go for a walk in nature and say thank you, mentally, for everything you see, hear or experience. For example: the warm sun, the crisp air, the gentle rain, the song of a bird, a beautiful tree or a plant that you see.

EXERCISE: *Thank-you Meditation*
This is about counting your blessings. Prepare by writing down every blessing you have in your life. Remember water, food, love, friendships, your body and senses, as well as material gifts.

1. Find somewhere you can be still and undisturbed.
2. Light a candle.
3. Close your eyes, and breathe deeply until you feel relaxed.

4. Picture all the good things in your life and say thank you for them.
5. Open your eyes.

EXERCISE: *Thank-you for Your Health*

We tend to focus on what is *not* working in our body. Some people can let a toe-ache dominate their day. Others have major physical problems, which tend to become overwhelming. Whatever we think about magnifies, so we can energise ill health by giving it attention.

When we meditate on and give thanks for everything in our body that is functioning well, our body responds positively. Gratitude is a route to health and healing.

1. Find somewhere you can be still and undisturbed.
2. Light a candle.
3. Close your eyes, and breathe deeply until you feel relaxed.
4. Focus on every part of your body that is comfortable and working well, and thank it.
5. Open your eyes.

EXERCISE: *Water Blessing*

Write the word 'love' or 'thank you' on a piece of paper and stick it onto your water filter or a jug of water. Leave it overnight and know that in the morning the crystals within the water will be full of vitality.

EXERCISE: *Gratitude*

This is an exercise to get in touch with all those things in our lives that we very often take for granted. It is a way of showing gratitude for these things.

A very good way to connect with how thankful you are for something, is to imagine your life without it. Don't dwell on it, but for a second or two picture living without sight, for instance.

Have a note book and for thirty days list five new items for which you are grateful – yes, that is five NEW things each day. Spend a few minutes thinking about each thing and what it really means to you. These things can be physical, emotional, or spiritual, for instance: your eyesight, your home or your ability to sense angels. When Shaaron is doing soul readings for people, she looks out over the lovely view of a garden, but she imagines what it would be like if she were looking at a brick wall or at traffic streaming by on a busy road, and is even more thankful for what she has.

After the thirty days, note down two things each day – you can now start to repeat items if necessary. Make this a daily habit for the rest of your life.

CHAPTER 10

The Energy Dome

The Intergalactic Council was aware of everything taking place within Atlantis and beyond. It wanted the conditions of the special experiment to be controlled and unique. So a vast umbrella of pure, high-frequency energy was placed over the continent, creating a biosphere within which elements and atmosphere could be controlled. One of its original functions was to regulate the weather over the five islands. Its power was such that there were no earthquakes and any storms remained outside the dome. The Intergalactic Council could change the frequency of any part of the system to allow rain to fall in measured amounts in different places. Perfect local eco-climates were created for each area.

The energy dome also acted as a protective bubble, for Atlantis was deliberately set apart from the rest of the world and had no communication with it. From the outer world, no one could sail through the invisible barrier into the islands and it was so programmed that if an Atlantean went near the boundary he would instinctively turn back. Of course, this meant that the spiritual technology available on Atlantis was not accessible to the other cultures on Earth. It is this which renders Atlantis so extraordinary.

Powering Atlantis

The energy blanket was something like our current ozone layer, but it was also an electricity network and a spiritual internet. It was created in the following way.

The Great Crystal, a huge generator like the mainframe of a computer, was linked to a network of crystal pyramids. These were located in the atmosphere high above the world, and floated in a triangular formation creating a grid of magnetic energy. Each pyramid had a large crystal on top of it, acting like a satellite computer, and was held in position by high-frequency energy flowing up through the centre of the pyramid. These large crystals acted like spiritual sub-stations to the main power station and were also generators in their own right.

The pyramids were antennae that sent signals throughout Atlantis to cells that needed to be powered. The modern equivalent would be the mobile phone system: a series of masts cover an area, acting as antennae for radio signals, and radiate signals to the phones. As you move with your phone towards the limit of the range of a mobile phone mast, it picks up the signals from the next one. The only difference is that the radio signals used now are highly dangerous, affecting the cellular structure of humans; most particularly children. In Atlantis, the Great Crystal and the pyramid crystals received their power from Source, so the current radiated was totally pure. These crystals composed the material of the invisible dome and this global grid of magnetic energy was used to power Atlantis and to keep the planet on its orbital path. They also formed a grid equivalent to our electricity system today. People could plug into it to draw their energy requirements, where the crystals formed the plugs. And if you lifted the bonnet of a transporter to look at the engine, you would find only a crystal.

On the ground, large crystals could draw on the force from the global grid for lighting, heating, transport or any other need. They also acted as batteries in which energy was stored. For example, the crystal within a transport vehicle would resonate with the crystal above the nearest pyramid, which would charge it. You could even programme a crystal to help plants to grow. This programming resonated and worked with the voltage of the energy dome. Among other things, these generator crystals were also used for teleportation: the ability to move through time and space and rematerialise somewhere else. Atlanteans were only able to use these crystals by maintaining their pure high vibration.

Spiritual purity was the key to the power of Atlantis

Nothing was wasted on the planet. If it could not be recycled back to the Earth, it was dematerialised and returned to pure energy. The trained priests had powers to draw in metals, materials and objects from other planets. These had the durability to last forever, so when their service was over they were returned to the universe. The power of the crystal grid was also used for this dematerialisation.

BIRTH CRYSTALS

At birth, each person brought with them crystals, which resonated with their planet of origin – however far away. If someone wanted to connect with the feeling of home on Orion, for example, or to a star 50,000 light years away, they plugged their birth crystals into the crystal grid to boost the signal and enable them to make the connection. They were not aware that they were doing this nor did they have a conscious communication with their loved ones at home, but when they worked with their birth crystals in this way they had an enhanced sense of wellbeing and peace. In a similar way, someone now might hold a particular crystal in her hand and say, 'I don't know why it is, but I always feel better when I touch this crystal.' Unconscious forces come into play.

THE GREAT CRYSTAL

The Great Crystal was also an interdimensional portal, which acted like a motorway into the cosmos. There were many junctions off it and roads led in all directions to different stars. Only the High Priests and Priestesses, and certain Magi, used this exit from Earth. They might travel along it, for example, if there was a meeting with the Great Council of Saturn.

Each of the twelve regions were linked to the Great Crystal and each other by ley lines, which were like major roadways. There were local roads, of course, and also main highways to the other regions. Above these were varying bands of energy frequency, along which people and transports could travel at different heights. The metal plates, used by children and adults to fly along the ley lines, were plugged into the main power grid. So were larger airbuses and even space ships, which were rarely used.

Those who had sufficient control of their energy fields spun an aerodynamic vortex around themselves to teleport along the motorways to the cathedral for meetings. They appeared in their full physical bodies to carry out their mission.

Crystal Pyramids

Most of the crystal pyramids no longer exist in our physical world, but they are still in place energetically, drawing people to them for magnetic initiation. When Atlantis sank, many of the pyramids were returned to the inner planes, but some do remain in the ether as spiritual homes of the masters and archangels. You can visit these in meditation or in dreams. These are a few of them:

* The spiritual home on Earth of Archangel Gabriel is in Mount Shasta, California.
* Sedona is an important power point, which attracts many people.

- Luxor, in Egypt, is the spiritual home of Serapis Bey, who was a High Priest at the spiritual height of Atlantis.
- The sacred mountains of Tibet hold wonderful magnetic energy, and you can connect with Djwhal Kuhl here. He is a great master who is currently in charge of the evolution of the planet.
- In the Gobi Desert is Shamballa, the retreat of the Illumined Masters and home of Sanat Kumara, who used to be the Planetary Logos, the boss of the universe and the greatest of the Avatars, who was in charge of the ascension process for the entire planet. He has now returned to Venus but still visits Earth, of course, and those who feel close to him can access his energy very strongly.
- The Royal Tetron Retreat in Wyoming. This ascension seat is physical and you can actually sit in it. However, you have to seek in the inner planes to be guided to it and receive permission to use it. You can also visit it in meditation and in your sleep time, as with the other retreats.

The above locations were not in Atlantis, but the crystal grid was a planet-wide system and used in a number of experiments for different reasons. One of these was, of course, to keep people within their own experiment so that they did not stray into the wrong one. Now the participants from all the experiments world-wide have mixed and interbred.

For aeons after the Intergalactic Council withdrew and allowed the people of Earth to do what they wanted without guidance, the planet was very dark. Now, however, people are becoming more spiritual and are asking for help again. Some of the portals are being reopened for us to access. The Himalayas, particularly, is once more becoming an area of light, where people can connect more readily to the divine. Currently the Intergalactic Council is contemplating bringing back the crystal pyramids as part of the 'quickening' of the planet on its rise to ascension.

EXERCISE: *Visit the Retreat of a Master or Archangel*
Read again the list of retreats of the masters and archangels, and choose one that intuitively calls you.

1. Sit quietly where you will be undisturbed.
2. If you are indoors, light a candle and dedicate it to the connection you are about to make. If you are outside, feel the energy of the sun and mentally make the same dedication.
3. Close your eyes and visualise an egg of golden Christ light surrounding you. The Christ light is one of the highest and purest energies of unconditional love.
4. With each out-breath, feel yourself relaxing and filling your aura with the colour gold.
5. Ask to be taken to the retreat you have chosen.
6. Be aware of a seemingly endless staircase, stretching out into the cosmos, and start to move up it.
7. Find yourself at the retreat and look around you.
8. Meet the master or archangel, and stay open for any communications.
9. Afterwards, thank the great Being and return down the staircase.
10. Open your eyes and feel your feet firmly on the ground.

CHAPTER 11

The Temples of Atlantis

The Temple of Poseidon

The Temple of Poseidon, sometimes known as the Cathedral of the Sacred Heights, formed one of the Seven Pillars of Wisdom, representing the Law of One. It was, of course, the most powerful place in the whole of Atlantis. It was named after Poseidon, who rules the sea, for the land was originally under the waves and was brought to the surface for the experiments. Ultimately it was returned to the ocean bed.

The oblong temple, which was 600 feet long, and 300 feet wide (182 by 92 metres), was constructed with no hard edges, according to sacred geometry and feng shui. It was built very simply of white, black and red local stone. The walls were covered with orichalcum, a pink-gold mountain copper, plentiful in the Atlantean Mountains, which made the cathedral shimmer in the sunlight as it perched above the plains of Atlantis. Metals and astrology are linked. The ions within the metals resonate with the movement of the planets with which they are associated. Orichalcum vibrates with the sun and this added to its power and might. It was used by the Incas and the Aztecs, and we understand that it can still be found in the Andes. Copper resonates with Venus and tin with Jupiter. Other metals are no longer available to us because they are from other worlds.

Metals like silver, gold, platinum and iron were developed later in Atlantis and were not used in the pure times. In later times it was the Magi, with their mighty power, who used alchemy to make gold from base metals. This, ultimately, became the metal of wisdom and enlightenment and was later placed by Thoth along the spokes of the planetary web of light to keep the vibration high in particular parts of the world.

The floor and internal walls of the temple were pure white marble and everything was softly rounded and clear cut. Nothing was decorated and adorned, except for appropriate crystals to raise the consciousness. A simple altar was the focus for spiritual services. In the centre of the cathedral was the most huge and awesome clear quartz crystal, the Great Crystal, which came from and was part of the Creator. It was a pure Source energy. There had been other enormous crystals created, one for each era.

The Sphinx

At the eastern gate of the cathedral was a gigantic statue of a sphinx, a unique representation of purity whose purpose was to be a source of power on Earth. It was made of material no longer on the planet. The sphinx represented the deity of Atlantis and contained the records for all the universes that ever have been, are and ever will be. These are known as the universal Akashic Records. This information was stored like books in a library, but the frequency was so high that only the High Priests and Priestesses could access it. Between the paws of the mighty creature in the Temple of Poseidon was a space, like a trapdoor, which was opened when the populace gathered below on ceremonial occasions. Then the Alta and the Initiates stood at the portal and channelled light onto the people. They bathed them in pure love, spiritual knowledge and healing to boost them and keep their frequency high. The great angels of Atlantis massed over the population during the ritual and 'held' the light for them.

Because everything was an equal exchange in Atlantis, the people then focused love and gratitude back to the rulers, which boosted their energy in return. As a coarse analogy, this acted in a similar way to the enthusiastic applause of an audience, which re-energises actors who have performed for their benefit. This energy exchange encouraged everyone to continue to work for the highest good of all and gave permission to the High Ones to take decisions on behalf of the people. The people had total faith in this.

The Sphinx of Egypt is the current earthly equivalent and contains the Akashic records for Earth. It was built at the start of the Age of Leo, the era of courage, beauty and love. Much older than scientists currently date it, it was originally painted red, symbolising the sacred warrior energy of its role as guardian of the planet. The Sphinx, when it had one hundred per cent of its power, sent out such pure and powerful light that it stopped invaders as they approached us. Because of the decline of spirituality on the planet, the Sphinx is currently almost power-less to protect Earth. It is vital that people worldwide, now focus on love, peace and light, thus enabling the Sphinx to regain its strength. When Diana's book, *The Web of Light*, was published, the life force of the Sphinx had reduced to two per cent. So many people have done the exercise in the book to energise the web of light over Africa, that within a few months its vitality had increased to five per cent. There is great hope for Earth if we all do our part.

INITIATION

The Temple of Poseidon contained the Great Initiation Chamber, where the Initiates were profoundly tested. To fail an initiation at this level could cause the soul to regress by hundreds of lifetimes. All the great beings who aspired to become High Priests and Priestesses had to undergo initiations in this chamber before they became part of the Alta. They were regularly challenged and even chose to face trials as a means of purifying themselves. Ultimately, the Intergalactic Council decided whether or not an applicant was formally accepted.

Those who aspired to become one of the Alta were highly-evolved beings, graduates of many of the most illustrious training establishments in the universes. For this experience, in addition to the formidable initiations they undertook before they were considered for this post, they were subject to a human body and all its trials and tests. The main reason for having a body was so that they could feel empathy with the populace, and could understand the problems and limitations of living in physical form.

Because of the Veil of Amnesia, the people who were incarnate in Atlantis were unconscious that they were participating in a divine experiment. The Alta, on the other hand, were aware, and this higher perspective allowed them to deal with matters, as they arose, with objectivity and wisdom.

Entry to the Temple of Poseidon was by levitation, so only Initiates and those who had mastered gravity and had control of their energy fields could go there. Only a very select few were ready to work in this elevated energy. And while the highly-trained senior priests could dematerialise and rematerialise themselves somewhere else, occasionally they needed to move the population en masse. At these times they conducted the people into huge teleportation chambers and rematerialised them in a different location. These teleportation chambers could only be operated by the High Priests, Priestesses and the Initiates.

ANNUAL CONNECTION WITH HOME

Once a year there was a ceremony for which every single person was gathered and taken to the Cathedral of the Sacred Heights. These ordinary people were only allowed in the main area and never entered the sacred central room. On this special occasion they were allowed the equivalent of an hour as we know it, to reconnect with their home planet. Of course, as third-dimensional beings, we understand time as linear and defined, whereas in Atlantis they did not have this limited concept. However, this special experience was a gift for taking part in the experiment of Atlantis and, for these precious moments, the Veil of Amnesia was lifted. It then was replaced, so they forgot, at a conscious level, what had happened, but the happy feeling remained. This still occurs today when we wake with a feeling of joy, but cannot recall where we have been in our dream.

This reward was offered annually for generations. Eventually, though, discontent surfaced as community on Atlantis started to break down. Some people had flashes or dreams of their home planets, which they did not understand. A few started to experience puzzling memories of their origin and this feeling that there was more to life than they understood added to their sense of disconnection. It became increasingly difficult to replace the Veil of Amnesia. But if people were to remember who they truly were, it would contravene the purpose of the experiment, which was to discover whether the volunteers could live in material frequencies and still maintain their oneness with Source. Eventually the privilege was discontinued and many suffered for the discontent of the few.

In later times, the pure simplicity of the great temple was lost as each successive High Priest and Priestess attempted to outdo his or her predecessor by improving it. Eventually, as Atlantis declined, it was adorned with precious metals, jewels and fabrics, and the leaders wore sumptuous, elaborately-decorated robes. The adage is 'Simple is spiritual, complexity is ego'.

Temples in the Twelve Regions

A temple was built on elevated ground in the centre of every town, for it was the focus of the community. Geomancy was considered important, so this special building was always the tallest and housed the master crystal for the region. These sacred buildings were round and painted with uplifting murals in glorious colours. The windows were of quartz crystal, which was plentiful and served to make the holy places even more special as ordinary houses had no windows.

All the elements were represented within the place of worship and oriented as the Native Americans still do: north for air, south for water, east for fire and west for earth. Only crystals were used to decorate the holy temples. These were placed in certain con-figurations, depending on the energy the High Priest or Priestess was trying to create for the community. Water was spiritually vital, so there were fountains inside the temple and the main building itself was surrounded by a canal. Beyond this was constructed a ring of houses, then another circle of running water, then another of dwellings, and so on, so their towns were built in concentric rings of homes, water, homes, water. The water was kept clean and pure and was used for recreation and bathing. Later, as commerce and profit entered the consciousness of Atlanteans, boatmen carried goods and plied their trades along these canals.

Naturally, when the communities were first designed and built, the homes were spaced well apart, amid tracts of greenery and clumps of trees.

Atlanteans considered the circle a symbol for understanding life's mysteries. The Earth is round, as are the sun, moon and planets. The rising and setting of the sun follows a circular motion; seasons form a circle; birds build round nests; animals mark their territories in circles. For this reason, the Atlanteans built circular homes.

ATLANTEAN COMMUNITIES

When a temple became too small for the town it served, the Mage was consulted. Another piece of high ground would be chosen

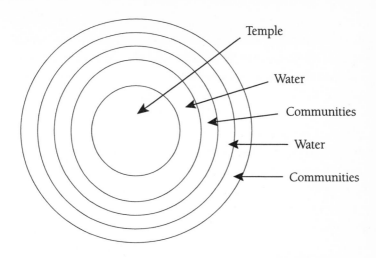

Layout of Atlantean Communities

and the sacred crystal from the centre of the temple moved there. Then the community constructed a fresh building round their crystal. The new centre would also include a school and healing rooms, as well as individual dream, sound and crystal chambers, which accommodated all skills. A bigger ring of houses would be constructed round it, incorporating the original town. The old temple would then be rededicated for teaching or healing and used accordingly.

In the beginning, the churches were very simply constructed and built of natural materials. Eventually, as the centuries passed, the main healing temple of Atlantis was circular, sixty feet (eighteen metres) in diameter, with a high-domed ceiling inlaid with crystals. It was beautifully decorated with gold.

As Atlantis expanded, the people needed to be balanced and healed. Temples of sound were created, which were circular and built to a specific height and width – the height being half the longest measurement. This meant that the pitch within was perfect. Sound was used for healing, regeneration of limbs, detoxification and to help maintain a high frequency. People also went to these healing sound chambers to align their chakras. It was in a temple of sound that each child received his travel plate so that he could fly above the ley lines.

> We are only now beginning to work with sound as the Atlanteans did, although our use of it is very elementary. For instance, we use the technology of sound for purposes such as the voices on voicemail messages, which are built of electronic signals.
> Today's knowledge is crude compared to that used in Atlantis.

In time there were dream temples, where people went to have dreams induced to give them information for healing. The priests developed dream catchers to help filter out nightmares and enable the dreamer to remember good dreams. The Native Americans still use these and for information on how to make your own dream catcher see Chapter 30. There were also temples that contained a variety of crystal rooms for specific purposes. For example, the marriage room was filled with selenite, as this crystal represents the marriage of spirit and matter. Where they performed the sun meditations, described later, the floor was made of hematite to keep them grounded.

As the temperature of Atlantis was controlled generally by the energy dome over the five islands, it was warmer in the south and cooler in the north. However, temperature could also be adjusted locally. Within each of the twelve main temples was an extra-ordinary instrument – something like a harp with thicker strings. It was made of luminescent, off-planet material. This instrument was used to affect the atmosphere, like a superior unit comprising air conditioning, central heating and humidifier in one. The priest would wave a crystal wand in front of it to change the thermostat and this would make the most incredible musical sound.

Although the music produced was not its primary purpose, the Atlanteans took every opportunity available to use the healing qualities of sound and water. It could also be used in the open to raise or lower the temperature – for example, if there was an outside party or gathering.

When Atlantis started to devolve, temples were more elaborately decorated and the clothing of the priests became richer. Some of them started to wear rings symbolising their marriage to God. As egos became entrenched, the priests wore headgear to indicate their level of seniority: the higher the hat, the loftier their position. This proclaimed they were more important than the masses. People lost their connection to nature and started to worship indoors, with services of supplication rather than thanksgiving. The principle of joy and manifestation through gratitude was lost.

EXERCISE: *20-Minute Ohm*
You can do this exercise on your own, but it is much more effective if you can do it with other people, especially sitting in a circle.

Ohm is a sacred and powerful sound, consisting of *Aah*, *oh* and *mm*. When it is sounded properly, it stimulates the third eye and crown. When *ohm*, *ohm*, *ohm* is chanted repeatedly for twenty minutes, every cell of the body is touched by the vibration. Twenty minutes seems a long time when you start, but as the sound flows through your body and into the room, raising your frequency, time disappears. When you are doing this exercise with a circle of people, everyone will have a slightly different breath length and so the effect will be of one continuous, circulating ohm.

1. Sit alone or in a circle with others. Let one person be the time keeper.
2. Place a lighted candle in the centre, or one in front of each

person.

3. Close your eyes and mindfully chant or say *ohm* in your own time. When you naturally reach the end of your ohm, take a breath and then chant ohm again.

4. Remain in silence when you have finished.

If you wish to, you can dedicate the sound to the manifestation of a personal wish, or something for the world as a whole.

CHAPTER 12

The Priesthood

Amongst the first 84,000 volunteers for Atlantis were those who carried the necessary skills and qualities to act as priests and priestesses. The twelve rulers, the Alta, picked out those who were naturally inclined to this role. Then they actively encouraged them to develop their gifts. All levels of the priesthood were the guardians of spirituality within Atlantis.

As soon as the second generation of immigrants arrived, the established priests and priestesses examined the auras of the children to discover their latent talents, which would be honoured and drawn out. They then chose and helped to develop future novices for the priesthood. Priests were male or female, for the Atlanteans knew they needed balance in the priesthood. They were also aware that men and women are equal parts of a pair. Priests and priestesses could marry and have families.

Only those who worked in the holy places were celibate and they lived in single accommodation within the temples, dedicating their lives to this purpose. Sex is predominantly a very earthy and grounding experience. Priests were trained to raise their sexual energy and use it in service to the Divine. They were honoured for their dedication. Remember, only those who were ready to use their sexuality in this way were allowed to do so and therefore it was never misused.

In the priesthood, different coloured garments were worn depending on their level. Novices were dressed in pale green,

Adepts in pale blue and Initiates in white robes. The Magi, who were incredibly highly trained shamans, and alchemists were attired in red-orange. The plain voluminous robes of the rulers were dark blue. There was no ego involved in this for no one was considered better than another. The only reason they wore different colours was for identification.

Training

The training for the priesthood was identical in each of the twelve regions of the continent.

NOVICES

For the first year of their training, at the age of thirteen, the Novices were taken out of the community completely. They stayed in seminaries attached to the temples, living in dormitories. Here they acquired self-discipline and were expected to display true compassion and empathy. They were trained to live in the moment and understand the power of it.

Eighty-five per cent of their time was spent in preparation to enter the silence, through chanting, meditation, visualisation and stillness. This state of grace enabled them to experience oneness. The other fifteen per cent of their time was spent learning about the energy fields and practising basic healing, mind control and realigning of the chakras. Those who trained them were carefully watching for their special skills, so that they could connect them to the spiritual levels where these could be developed.

The trainee priests were allowed to marry when they had finished the closeted part of their training in the first year. However, if they wished to become an Adept, they had to remain celibate until they had completed the appropriate training.

In the second year, they lived in the community again and were tested to see if they could maintain a level of stillness while out in the world. No one ever failed because they had been chosen for their spiritual qualities, and those who trained them knew they were meant to be priests. If there was a weakness, however, they were taught to turn it into a strength.

During this time they learnt more advanced healing techniques, basic crystal layouts and mind control. They were taught the power of gratitude and the skills of teleporting, telekinesis and levitation. They would learn more advanced mind control, for example: how to direct their energy to make their hands hot or to lower their temperature, or how to teleport a drinking vessel from one place to another.

Most important of all, they continued to prepare themselves to be vessels for higher energies. At this stage of their training they learnt that precipitation – which is the manipulation of pure energy into solid form – channelling and manifestation exist.

ADEPTS

The Adepts undertook a three-year training. The first year was in the temple and they did not emerge during this time. After that they lived within society. Initially their lessons included healing, geomancy – which we call feng shui – the leading of ceremonies and techniques to teach the Novices. They also started to learn to overcome gravity.

In the first year they chose a specialist skill to develop, based on the gifts they brought with them to Earth. Some became teachers or learned about crystal or spiritual healing. Others trained as counsellors and spiritual mentors, or temple workers.

In the second and third years of their course they combined experience with learning and worked under the direction of an Initiate. Teachers would be involved in the teaching temples. Spiritual counsellors could discuss imbalances within relationships or help families deal with emotions. Perfect health was considered the norm. This meant that in the early days there was nothing to heal and all that the healing priests had to do was to balance energy fields within individuals. Temple workers could preside over local ceremonies for funerals or the celebration of a birth and naming of a child. They also helped to train the Novices. There *were* married Adepts, but many were dedicated to celibacy. If they worked in the temples they were on duty twenty-four hours a day and their vocation became their whole life.

INITIATES

In order to become an Initiate, the Adept was challenged to complete certain tasks to prove his or her abilities. This was a rite of passage, but they were also assessed continuously throughout their training. Very few Adepts actually graduated to become an Initiate. No one could do so until he or she had demonstrated they could overcome gravity, for the power to fly granted them entry to the Temple of Poseidon. Initiates were highly advanced: they were expected to have complete mastery over their bodies, and to be able to control their heartbeat, sugar levels and temperature. They could also walk on nails or hot coals. These extraordinarily dedicated and highly spiritual beings had such total control of their energy fields that they could render themselves invisible. Initiates practised advanced levitation and were highly disciplined in mind control. They were also trained in soul retrieval. These evolved ones worked with the pyramid energy and helped to maintain the frequency of Atlantis. They also oversaw all the levels of priesthood and presided over certain ceremonies.

THE MAGI

A few of the most powerful, devoted and pure Initiates became Magi. They were extremely highly-trained scientists, alchemists, astrologers, astronomers, palmists and numerologists. They had the power to control the elements and were shamans, who practised necromancy, which involves conversing with the dead, soul retrieval, prophecy and divination. It was the Magi who could see clearly into the future. They were the ones who watched beyond our world and warned of attacks on Earth.

Shamans of all races have worn feathers since the beginning of time. To the Magi a feather was highly significant and they recognised that it gives out an impulse of high-frequency energy. It is also symbolic of angelic energy.

Like the Initiates, they practised soul retrieval and would find a lost soul, if it was cast adrift, and send it on its correct journey. In the golden years most people passed smoothly to their destination, so the service of the Magi was required only if there was an unexpected or painful death and the soul was shocked and disorientated. Such passings were usually as a result of accidents, but occasionally they arose from childbirth and might involve either the mother or the child. Of course, as we have already discussed, these were all souls that had elected to die in this manner to enable the remaining family or friends to experience emotions of loss, grief, fear, anger and other feelings associated with bereavement.

When their service to the planet was completed, the Magi went to specially-designated natural crystal chambers, where they vacated their bodies, never to return. They ascended to their home planets.

The training rendered Magi very powerful. For 1,500 years they dedicated this power in service to the highest good of all. However, it was they who ultimately caused the downfall of Atlantis by desiring to use the power for their own ego aggrandisement.

Those Initiates and Magi who maintained their integrity are now the teachers and counsellors in the spirit world, who help us to choose our next lives and train us between incarnations. They are the higher spirit guides and masters. The talents and gifts they practised in Atlantis are used today to help the world. And they will reincarnate when we on Earth are ready to bring back the purity and power of Golden Atlantis.

THE ALTA

The High Priests and Priestesses did not accept partners because all their energy was needed for their mighty tasks. There were twelve rulers: the Priest Kings and Queens, known as the Alta. They spent most of their time in the Temple, but they did have a residence within their home cities, rather like our politicians.

They maintained intergalactic contact, reporting on the progress of the Atlantis experiment to the Great Council and taking decisions with them about the future. One of their tasks was to keep the portal of the Great Crystal pure and protected. It was the High Priests and Priestesses who adjusted the levels and frequencies of the great biodome over the continent. They could not do these things individually, so they had to work in harmony and took collective decisions.

The Alta poured high-frequency light onto the populace on special occasions to keep the vibration of the people pure and they occasionally presided over important ceremonies, including those for the promotion of different levels of priests and to welcome the seasons.

The great High Priest, Thoth, channelled the Seven Spiritual Laws for Atlantis and a great many subsidiary laws. These were later simplified by Jesus into thirty-three spiritual laws, with three transcendent laws.

The High Priests and Priestesses were each responsible for their own tribes and managed them differently according to their individual energies. The Intergalactic Council originally decided to form twelve tribes so that it would give them multiple chances to get the experiment right.

Mind Control

There are many practical applications of this skill, including altering your blood pressure, changing your sugar levels and your temperature. Mind control is mainly used today in pain relief and sleep enhancement. It is, of course, a basic aspect of deep meditation and absent healing. The ancient abilities of fire-walking, sitting on beds of nails or sleeping in freezing conditions – which have traditionally been practiced in the East – are now being demonstrated in the West. Here is one example that you can try for yourself:

EXERCISE: *Mind Control – Altering the Temperature*
We all have power to control our temperature, but it takes mind focus.

1. Notice the temperature and colour of your hands.
2. Close your eyes and focus all your attention on your right hand. Imagine it immersed in a bowl of comfortably-hot water. Take time to sense the temperature. Feel your pores opening and your hand becoming warm.
3. Focus your attention on your left hand. Imagine it immersed in a bowl of iced water. Sense the temperature. Imagine the lumps of ice touching your skin. Feel your hand becoming colder.
4. Open your eyes. Note how your hands feel and examine the colour.

Practise this exercise until you really can change the temperature of your hands.

CHAPTER 13

The High Priests
and Priestesses

During the Golden Age many great beings came to Earth to experience physical incarnation and undergo the training to become Initiates or High Priests and Priestesses. Of the latter, there were always twelve at any given time. As Atlantis evolved, suitable beings who had the knowledge, wisdom and experience appropriate to command the experiment at that time were invited to take on this role. Among them were Hercules, Pallas Athena, who was a High Priestess in the Temple of Truth, and Lady Portia, known as the Goddess of Justice.

These Wise Ones had powers and abilities almost beyond our comprehension. Take, for example, Thoth, one of the first High Priests. He was aware that our planet had, in ancient times, collided with another planet and when they finally separated Earth had taken all the minerals of both. This means that we are extremely rich in metals and minerals. Molten metal within the Earth generates a current that produces a magnetic field. Using his powers, Thoth channelled this force into straight lines to create an energy grid around the planet. It was much easier for people to travel in the air above these power lines and they used them as aerial roadways.

The Twelve Rays

In Atlantean times there were twelve rays, each of which shines a divine quality onto Earth. Each ray carries a different frequency and various colours and qualities that affect the population of our planet. As Atlantis lost its purity and the power was misused, the higher five rays, known as the Master Rays, were gradually withdrawn leaving seven focused on Earth. In recent years, the frequency of humanity and Gaia herself has been rising again and in 2001, the Intergalactic Council agreed that the energy of the eighth and ninth rays could be directed here once more so that everyone could benefit. The tenth, eleventh and twelfth rays followed in the next two years. Diana and Shaaron's guide Kumeka, is the Master of the Eighth Ray. He was not incarnate in Atlantis, but was one of the very high beings from the spiritual world who had a supervisory role. Each of the other current Chohans or Masters of the Twelve Rays had incarnations in Atlantis.

MASTERS OF RAYS

Ray 1. El Morya is the Chohan of the First Ray of Power, Will and Purpose. At the fall of Atlantis, he carried its knowledge and wisdom to the Euphrates and was instrumental in establishing the Mesopotamian civilisation. He oversaw the development of their script so that they could keep records on clay tablets. He also helped to develop the Islamic faith and its art. He originates from Mercury.

Ray 2. Lanto is the Chohan of the Second Ray of Love and Wisdom. He was the great Chinese philosopher of the same name; during this incarnation he developed unconditional love to such an extent that golden light shone from his heart centre. After that, he oversaw the development of one of Earth's twin planets, which is more evolved than we are. A mighty being indeed!

Ray 3. Paul the Venetian, known as Master Paul, is now the Chohan of the Third Ray of Intelligence and Creative Activity. He served in Government as Head of Cultural Affairs in Atlantis.

Ray 4. Serapis Bey, who originated from Venus, is the Chohan of the Fourth Ray of Harmony and Balance. He was a great Priest, Avatar, in Atlantis, and Keeper of the White Flame. Now he is often known as The Egyptian because at the fall of Atlantis he worked with Metatron and the angels to influence the building of the Pyramids, where his teachings are said to be hidden.

Ray 5. Master Hilarion is currently the Chohan of the Fifth Ray of Science, Wisdom and Knowledge. He worked in the Temple of Truth in Atlantis. The capital of the solar system is on Saturn and he is still the negotiator for Earth on the Council of Saturn.

Ray 6. Mary Magdelene has become Chohan of the Sixth Ray of Idealism and Devotion. In the New Age her role is to break down the walls of dogma in people's minds and bring back the true spirituality as it was understood in Atlantis.

Ray 7. Lady Nada has taken over the Seventh Ray of Ritual, Ceremony and Magic. She still sits on the board of the Lords of Karma, and was a Priestess in the Temple of Love, in Atlantis.

Ray 8. This is the Ray of Deep Transmutation. Kumeka, Lord of Light, is the Chohan of this ray. He comes from another universe to help us prepare ourselves and the Earth for our ascension into higher spiritual frequencies. He was one of those who played a major role in the development of the golden years of Atlantis.

Ray 9. Vosloo is the Chohan of the Ninth Ray of Harmony, which aims to balance the mind and spirit of humanity. He was one of the most evolved High Priests in Atlantis and, as a result of his service, he understands what went wrong and is now dedicated to ensuring that we do not make the same mistakes again. He was also deeply connected with Egypt.

Ray 10. Lord Gautama, who later became the Buddha, is Chohan of the Tenth Ray of Peace and Wisdom, which enables people to find their practical purpose in life, in a grounded way, and carries the Buddha energies. He was Thoth in Atlantis.

Ray 11. Rakoczy, who incarnated as St Germain, is the Chohan of the Eleventh Ray of Clarity, Mysticism and Healing. He was a High Priest in Atlantis.

Ray 12. Quan Yin, who is the eastern counterpart of Mother Mary, is the Chohan of the Twelfth Ray of Unconditional Love. She currently represents the sixth ray on the Karmic Board, which watches over and governs karma on the planet. In Atlantis, and later in China, she was known as the Goddess of Mercy.

When you read or speak aloud the names of these Illumined Ones, a high-frequency wave of light automatically flows through you. It provides nourishment for your soul. When you invoke each of them aloud, it gives you a great spiritual boost, as it draws their blessing and the light of their ray to you. We give two possible invocations at the end of the chapter.

The Evolution of the Twelve

Of the twelve High Priests or Priestesses, six were connected to the energy that would later become Greece and in due course became Greek Gods, and the remaining six were connected with the future Egypt and later were revered as Egyptian Gods.

The original twelve High Priests and Priestesses were chosen for their ability to nurse and encourage people through the initial stages of a project. As a comparison, when we start our education at primary level we have teachers specifically trained to work with our age group. When we move into junior and senior school, then university and even post-graduate training, we receive our education from those who have the appropriate qualifications. So it was in Atlantis.

The first twelve were elementary teachers. During the evolution of Atlantis, the Council would change the leaders to bring in new energies and learning. At the pinnacle of the evolution extremely high cosmic masters were invited to take on the role of High Priests and Priestesses. They were like college lecturers compared with the infant teachers. One of these graduate-level educators was Voosloo, who has now returned as Master of the Ninth Ray. After Atlantis reached its peak of spiritual development and started to devolve, appropriate High Priests and Priestesses were appointed according to their level of light. By the time the experiment terminated, the whole world was back at a primary level. So those High Priests and Priestesses who were there at the beginning were sent back to Atlantis to take the tribes from the doomed continent. They had the perfect experience and energy to lead the survivors out into the unknown world. Their aim was to reintroduce simplicity. They led their tribes to various specially-prepared places, which we discuss later. Once there, they helped them to settle into their new lives at a lower frequency.

Those who were there at the beginning and end of this phase of Atlantis were Thoth, Isis, Horus, Ra, Sett and Imhotep. They were connected to Egypt. Hermes, Zeus, Aphrodite, Apollo, Poseidon and Hera were linked to Greece. Where they took their tribes, and the wisdom they carried with them, are discussed in a later chapter.

EXERCISE: *Invoking the Power of One Master of the Rays*
1. Intuitively choose one of the Masters of the Rays.
2. Sit quietly, with your eyes closed, and invoke him or her –
   aloud if possible or silently if not. To do this verbally or

mentally say, for example: 'I now invoke the mighty Isis and ask you to touch me with your energy'.

3. Feel their energy surrounding you and make yourself open to receiving any information or guidance.
4. When you have finished, close down by touching each of your chakras in turn. Seal them by drawing a cross over each one with your finger. Then make sure you are grounded by visualising roots going down into the earth.
5. Write down what you experienced or felt.

As you continue to record your experiences, you will notice how they change and deepen.

EXERCISE: *Invoking the Power of All the Masters*
Before invoking all the Masters, make sure you have enough time!

1. Sit quietly, with the book open in front of you, or make a list of the Illumined Ones of Atlantis.
2. Invoke each one aloud or silently. Use the formula: 'I now invoke the mighty (insert name) and ask you to fill me with your energy'.
3. After each invocation, allow yourself time to absorb the energy and feelings.
4. When you have finished, close down, and make sure you are grounded as outlined in the previous exercise.
5. Write down what you experienced or felt.

CHAPTER 14

Atlantean Energies

The Violet Flame

In the previous, failed, experiments on Atlantis, the majority of settlers had been overcome with their own and other people's dark thought forms. These were like clouds, which penetrated people's auras and profoundly affected them. Eventually the Intergalactic Council decided to give them something that would transmute the dire negativity. They offered the Violet Flame, which was composed of light so pure that it could dissolve the particles of fear and anger emitted by almost everyone. The flame was composed of shades from lavender, through lilac, to deepest violet and had to be invoked when required.

In view of their past experiences, the Council decided to retain the Violet Flame for the new experiment in case it should be needed. Of course, at first the people of the golden times kept themselves in balance and lived harmonious lives. Nevertheless, with a physical body, relationships and emotions to deal with, there were inevitably negative thoughts flying about from time to time.

When darkness is merely banished, it is still alive and can affect or infect others. Negativity needs to be transformed into something positive: sickness into health; poverty into plenty, jealousy into self-esteem, greed into generosity and despair into hope. The people were taught to cancel negative energy in the Violet Flame and replace it with a positive one. Because they were clairvoyant, they could see any dark patches of stuck emotions in their friends' auras, and could call on the Violet Flame to transmute it into something helpful. In this way they served each other.

If someone sent out a little snake of jealousy or an angry cord, it was impossible to hide this. Families kept themselves and each other pure and uncontaminated by dissolving such thoughts in the Violet Flame and replacing them with love and light. They could use the flame to dissolve any pains in their bodies, or those of their friends, or to heal disharmony in relationships. Because they practised mind control and were conscious of every thought or feeling that arose, it was relatively easy to keep their energy fields clear with the help of the Violet Flame.

Like all powerful energies this one could be abused and indeed it was in later Atlantis until it was withdrawn. For thousands of years, we on Earth have struggled with our darker emotions without this wonderful tool – until recently. At the Harmonic Convergence in August 1987, so many lightworkers prayed for planetary healing that St Germain approached Source and asked for a dispensation. As a result, after 12,000 years, the Violet Flame was returned to us for our use. Because lightworkers continued to devote themselves to raising the frequency of the planet, a further divine clemency was granted in 1998. The Silver Ray of Grace and Harmony was merged with the Violet Flame of Transmutation. It was a great gift to humanity.

When you invoke the Silver Violet Flame, negative energy is transmuted and automatically replaced with something of a higher frequency.

Mahatma Energy

This is a high-frequency, golden-white, cosmic energy, made up of a group consciousness consisting of the twelve rays, Buddha energy, Christ energy, that of the Spirit of Peace and Equilibrium, and other vast cosmic beings, which formed in Atlantean times to help the priests when things started to go wrong. It was a dispensation granted by Source to help the experiment. The intention was that if invoked, it would keep the priests pure so that they in turn could keep the populace pure. It acted as a boost of high-frequency energy running through their mental, emotional, spiritual and physical bodies. When the Atlanteans invoked the golden-white energy, it flowed through the different levels of their auras and into the earth, breaking up hard, crystallised thought forms and emotional patterns as it did so. Therefore, it helped personal problems and could be sent to others for healing and to resolve situations. It had amazing healing energy and could help to re-energise the glands, keep the people youthful and sexually alive, balance the metabolism, and strengthen the immune system. Spiritually, it built their light-bodies quickly and accelerated their ascension process.

Later in Atlantis, the Mahatma Energy was abused in the same way as the Violet Flame and withdrawn. The people were told that it would be returned when Earth was ready. Again, as a result of the prayers of humanity at the Harmonic Convergence in 1987, it was made available to humanity again. It is the highest energy that can be accessed by humans at present and accelerates the path to ascension one-thousandfold. It can be accessed by anyone but, as with all things spiritual, you must ask for it.

The Mahatma Energy desires to be anchored as much as possible on Earth right now, for humans are a bridge between Source and Earth.

The Great Pool of Pure Energy

The High Priests and Priestesses created a pool of pure energy, which was incredibly powerful and increased and purified anything it touched. The people could access it in order to help with healing, manifestation, transportation and precipitation. When they invoked this energy, it added power wherever it was directed. The energy was similar to that used by the great biodome. The power of the Golden Age was its purity. Nothing existed except as pure energy. The frequency in Atlantis was so high that, through the power of their minds, everyone could use the energy from the Great Pool and precipitate it into material form. In the early days, the Magi had the right and the power to use this energy in its entirety and they did so with integrity. It was as if the people could plug in a sixty-watt bulb and the trained Initiates a 1,000-watt bulb. They all knew how to employ the power wisely.

The people used it to create buildings, roads, swimming pools, transporters or anything they needed for the highest good. They accessed energy from the Great Pool and shaped it with artistic flair. Everything they created had grandeur and style un-imaginable to us now.

It was when a Mage realised that this energy could be accessed for personal use, that the experiment started to deteriorate. Until that time there had been only highly-evolved angels of light in Atlantis. They were of a much lighter frequency than the guardian angels now delegated to look after us. At the moment that the Mage used the pure power for ego aggrandisement, the first dark angel gained entry to the continent.

At last, the energy of healers, spiritual teachers, lightworkers and people offering prayers is starting to recreate the reservoir of light. The Intergalactic Council is watching our efforts and mighty beings in the inner planes are being attracted to help this process.

The Gem Rays

In Atlantis, as now, the mighty Archangels Michael, Uriel, Raphael and Gabriel poured their rays onto Earth and helped to light the way for the people. Not only did they radiate down their special energy, but they also materialised it into solid form under the ground to help the planet and energise the ley lines.

- The dark blue light of Archangel Michael's ray created the sapphire.
- The purple and gold light of Archangel Uriel's ray; the ruby.
- The brilliant green light of Archangel Raphael's ray; the emerald.
- The pure white light of Archangel Gabriel's ray; the diamond.

Many other archangels light up and influence crystals. For example, the energy of Archangel Zadkiel, the mighty angel of transmutation and mercy, formed the amethyst. His divine partner, or twin flame, is known as Lady Amethyst. And Archangel Chamuel, angel of love, works with the rose quartz, which helps to soften barriers round people's hearts and fill them with love.

In early Atlantis, when life was simple, the people wore one single crystal or gem, attuned to raise their consciousness. As the experiment began to deteriorate, the more sophisticated individuals adorned themselves with a great deal of jewellery. The precious gems raised the frequency of the wearer allowing direct connection with the archangels, thereby conferring that power.

Unfortunately, these later Atlanteans had devolved to the point where they were corrupted by this power. Also at this time, precious jewellery added to the status and prestige of those who wore them, for only the rulers and people of wealth and influence could afford to do so. In current times, rich people still wear these gems, unconsciously realising that they attune them to great power. Those who use this power wisely benefit from it.

The Sapphire. The sapphire enhances the wearer's power and strength and also enables him or her to communicate clearly, both telepathically and verbally. The stone holds within it ancient knowledge, which the owner can access to bring forward his own wisdom. The energy of the gem is balanced and softened by the influence of Archangel Michael's twin flame, Lady Faith, who adds the wisdom of the Divine Feminine.

The Ruby. This is a regal stone, for the purple within it contains royal blue, red and gold. This gives the wearer power to take action decisively, yet with wisdom and natural grace. Aurora, the twin flame of Archangel Uriel, brings peace and serenity, enabling creative ideas to evolve and blossom for those attracted to this stone.

The Emerald. Archangel Raphael has poured his divine light of trust, healing and wisdom into this stone, which has the power to take people to a high level of spirituality. His twin flame, Mother Mary, Queen of Angels, adds her qualities of love and compassion, so this is worn by leaders who are heart centred.

The Diamond. The diamond symbolises purity, eternity, clarity, truth and honour, which is why – even now – it is often chosen for engagement rings. Archangel Gabriel uses this energy to cut through illusion and take people into the higher dimensions. His twin flame, Hope, adds rainbows of joy.

The Platinum Ray. This is the ray of joy and bliss, representing a perfect balance of masculine and feminine. The dolphins are attuned to this ray, which connects them to the higher energies of the galaxy. They are the keepers of the sacred wisdom of Atlantis and are now seeking people who are pure and evolved enough to take back the ancient knowledge and reveal it to humanity.

EXERCISE: *The Silver Violet Flame*
You can do this as a meditation or when you are taking a walk or gardening, but not when you are driving a car or operating

machinery. This is a high spiritual energy, which opens you up, so ask Archangel Michael to place his deep-blue cloak of protection around you, and visualise it surrounding your body.

1. Mentally invoke the Silver Violet Flame. Visualise a flame of lilac, lavender, purple, violet and silver surrounding you.
2. Picture the Silver Violet Flame blazing a trail in front of you during the day, dissolving any dark energy before you encounter it.
3. Send the flame to people who are sick. See it consuming any negativity around them.
4. Place your anger or fear, hurt or negativity in the flame until they dissolve.
5. Picture people who are not in harmony, inside the flame.
6. Visualise the flame travelling, or ask the angels to take it to places to purify the energy of war and disruption.
7. If you have any pain or tension in your body, allow the Silver Violet Flame to play in that area.
8. Send it down phone lines or the internet to purify the web.
9. When you have finished place a cross or other symbol of protection in front and behind to close down your chakras.

EXERCISE: *The Mahatma Energy*
1. Close your eyes and relax.
2. Ground yourself by imagining roots going into the Earth.
3. Invoke the Mahatma Energy. Visualise a golden-white stream of light coming down into your crown. Allow it to bathe, soothe, balance and energise each of the glands in turn
   - The pineal gland at the crown, which emits and absorbs lights and keeps us in divine harmony.
   - The pituitary gland at the third eye: the master gland, that of eternal life.
   - The thyroid at the throat chakra, which governs the metabolism and production of antibodies.

- The thymus at the heart chakra, which governs the immune system.
- The pancreas at the solar plexus, which deals with sugar and nourishment, enabling us to absorb emotional and mental sweetness.
- The gonads, the ovaries and the testes at the sacral chakra, which govern the sexual and reproductive organs of the body.
- The adrenals at the base chakra, which send out adrenaline in response to the fight or flight mechanism of the body and gets rid of rubbish.

4. Let the Mahatma Energy flow through you into the Earth.
5. Picture a problem or difficult situation in your life and visualise the Mahatma Energy flowing through it, breaking up the old vibration.
6. Visualise a world problem and see the Mahatma Energy flowing through it and dissolving the old vibration.

EXERCISE: *Connect with Gems*
If you have a piece of jewellery containing one of the gems, that is wonderful. Hold it for this exercise. If not, don't worry – your heart and mind will tune you in.

First decide whether you wish to connect to the energy of the diamond, the ruby, the emerald or the sapphire. Prepare a place where you can be quiet and still. Light a candle, play soft music, and light an incense stick if you wish to.

1. Sit comfortably and breathe yourself into a relaxed state.
2. Imagine that you are walking into a secluded grove. Beautiful trees encircle a grassy centre and there is a stream nearby. You have a feeling of total safety and security.
3. As you stand there waiting, you may be aware of the flowers and smell their perfume. Notice any animals or birds that are

peacefully waiting. Listen to the tinkling stream and see how it sparkles and twinkles in the sunlight.

4. In the centre of the circle, a huge gem is manifesting. It is taller than you and transparent in its luminosity.

5. Walk towards it and touch it. See how each facet is clear cut and shining.

6. Find yourself inside the gem. Experience its energy.

7. And now, the mighty archangel is with you, raising your frequency, and giving you a message.

8. The archangel and the gem are fading away and you spend a few minutes in the grove, considering what you have experienced and learnt.

9. Open your eyes and write down what you wish to remember.

CHAPTER 15

Genetic Healing

The people of Atlantis, living at a fifth-dimensional frequency, worked with twelve chakras or spiritual energy centres. When our spiritual connection lessened, during the fall of Atlantis, the three upper chakras fell dormant. These three chakras – the stellar gateway, the soul star and the causal chakra – emit very different states of consciousness from the chakras we know today. At that time the people had longer heads and larger brains than we have currently. Their heads were elongated at the back, as we see in ancient Egyptian pictures. Some babies are now being born with this head structure and are bringing back ancient possibilities of those times when they used ninety per cent of their expanded brain capacity. Today we use ten per cent of our much smaller brain and it is time to develop this.

As humans became self-centred, the focus turned to their physical body rather than their spiritual connection. Pain, loneliness and separation were the consequences of increased ego. And as people's energy was used for the satisfaction of individual desires and personal prestige, pure energy became clouded. In earlier times people glowed with life force; now it dimmed so that their energy became grey and shadowy. As long as there are lessons to learn on the physical plane, it is not possible to connect with these higher chakras. However, many spiritual people have learnt their lessons and balanced their karma. Furthermore, the more people who do move forward and upward now, the more quickly others will follow suit.

We have continued to devolve since the fall of Atlantis, so five of the twelve chakras have closed and their connections are currently unavailable to us. We are now operating a seven-chakra system, but this is about to change since our DNA complex is intimately connected with our chakras.

DNA

The Atlanteans knew how to relax every part of their bodies, right down to the cells, and this is how they maintained their powers and their divine connections. Every cell within us is a little world of its own. Within the nucleus of each one, in the chromosomes, the DNA is found. DNA is a molecule in the shape of a double helix, and looks similar to two chains of beads wrapping round each other like snakes. There are thousands of genes within each double helix of DNA and they give instructions to our cells to carry out essential body functions, like breathing, where they send instructions to the autonomic nervous system. They also contain the codes that decide our physical make-up, for example: our eye colour, the thickness of our hair or a predisposition to certain illnesses. Every single cell in our body contains the genetic code for our entire body. Your own particular genetic coding is, of course, a spiritual decision taken before birth, depending on your karma and what challenges or lessons your soul wishes to undertake. But it can be profoundly affected by the way you live your life as well as by thoughts and emotions.

Scientific experiments have discovered that when feelings of love, peace, joy, gratitude and appreciation were focused onto vials containing DNA, the snakes or strands of beads uncoiled, stretched out, relaxed and connected. When researches projected anger, fear, frustration or stress onto it, the strands tightened and wound up. The codons or beads also went out of synch and separated, only touching at intervals, so that some of the amino acids were not formed. This is a bit like receiving a programme on a radio that has a loose connection or is improperly tuned in, and has vital implications for our immune systems and our spiritual lives.

Consequently, when the strands tightened as the purity of Atlantis was clouded, many of the codes within the DNA that dictate our genetic make-up automatically switched off. As this happened our psychic and spiritual abilities were disconnected.

These codes – or building blocks of life – consist of sixty-four possible combinations of oxygen, hydrogen, carbon and nitrogen. However, today, only twenty are enabled, while the remaining forty-four are dormant. Forty-four is the number that represents the wisdom of pure Atlantis: it indicates spiritual purity. What is the true purpose of the other forty-four codes? And how can we turn them on again? How can we regain the full twelve strands of DNA that we had in Atlantis?

In sacred Atlantis, although everyone had twelve strands of DNA within each cell, even then the true divine clarity was clouded because they went through the Veil of Amnesia in order to remain rooted in their physical bodies and to react to their environment through their physicality.

When we switch the disconnected codes on again we regain our full twelve strands of DNA and this allows us to merge with the oneness. These disconnected codes contain our psychic and spiritual gifts, telepathy, telekinesis, powers of manifestation, clairvoyance, clairaudience, self-healing and all the powers that await us. Reconnecting with the codes will bring back all the genetic information from all previous lives; this lifts the Veil of Amnesia and brings to us everything that we ever have been and will be. We do this by raising our frequency with love and by relaxing deeply. Then it will all happen automatically.

Incidentally, psychic children who are now being born with

twelve strands of DNA cannot use it because the atmosphere is too dense, so they demonstrate with such conditions as autism. As we clean up the planet and raise the frequency, 'cures' for autism will be found, but in fact it will be the raising of the frequency that enables autistic people to use their potential fully. People often ask us how they can best help their crystal or indigo offspring or autistic children. On a spiritual level, the greatest gift you can offer them is to purify yourself and raise your frequency. You do this, of course, by self-healing, forgiveness and by choosing peace and love at all times.

Bursts of cosmic energy are being sent through now by the Intergalactic Council that will allow those who are spiritually ready to reactivate the upper chakras and expand their consciousness. At last it is possible that the twelve chakras can be returned to humanity and the twelve strands of DNA can be switched on again. The keys are love, compassion, empathy, joy, generosity and positive living. But they must be combined with a relaxed, contemplative enjoyment of life.

White Powder Gold

As the spiritual purity of Atlantis declined, the Magi wished to retain their psychic abilities. By process of alchemy, they created white powder gold, which enabled the pineal gland to work at a high frequency and enhanced awareness, perception and intuition. It also fed the light-body. In later times this white powder gold was ingested by the Pharoahs to keep their energy clear and attuned.

This powdered metal is now available to us once more, but it can only be taken with impunity by highly-evolved souls. Right now humanity is not evolved or responsible enough to deal with the consequences of taking it, for it enhances whatever is dominant in the person's characteristics and personality. If someone had psychopathic tendencies, for example, it would accentuate them; a warrior spirit who strives to get things done his way would become even more centred and ego-driven; a flaky person would become more ungrounded. Of course, if the Dalai Lama took it, it would enhance his spirituality.

Genetic History

When a male deposits his sperm inside a female, his whole genetic history is joined to the female's. The reason for this is because the child to be created needs both the mother's and the father's story line. Mating is taking two halves and making them whole.

After she has given birth, or as soon as she is aware that the union has not resulted in fertilisation, the woman needs to visualise the sperm leaving her body. (This refers to the energy, of course, not the physical matter.) Sometimes the female holds on to the energy of the sperm and therefore takes in the man's genetic information and absorbs it into her being. Females whose identity comes through their man, women who love too much and prostitutes all tend to hold on. That is the woman's choice but it debilitates her and can contribute to illness – sometimes cancer. Kumeka says that the incidence of illness could be decreased significantly by women actively doing meditations to release all past connections with sexual partners.

Obviously, you would not do this visualisation if you are trying to get pregnant. And, of course, however much you love your partner, this is not about letting him go. It is about releasing the burden of his genetic karma that you have absorbed and self-purification.

EXERCISE FOR WOMEN:
Release the Energy of Sexual Partners
1. Close your eyes and relax.
2. Picture the man with whom you have had sexual
   intercourse. If you cannot do this for any reason, just think

about it.

3. Sense or imagine the energy of the sperm, containing his entire genetic history, like frogspawn or jelly inside you.
4. Imagine it all being washed away. Every single last bit.
5. Visualise yourself standing under a shower and being cleansed from head to toe.
6. Visualise a pure white angel of light placing a white robe on you to symbolise purification and release.

EXERCISE: *Connecting with your DNA*
1. Relax as deeply as you can by focusing on your breathing.
2. In your mind's eye, imagine one cell of your body. In it are two double strands of beads (two double helixes). Are they relaxed or wound up?
3. Imagine the cell being filled with golden light. Breathe love and gratitude into it.
4. Watch it expand and the two double strands of beads stretch out, just like a person lying on a beach on a warm sunny day.
5. Let more double strands of beads join the two, until there are twelve – all relaxed and comfortable.
6. Ask the twelve to work together to bring you healing, peace and enlightenment.
7. Close down and open your eyes.

Remember that your cells communicate with each other, and every time you do this exercise they send healing, peace, love and higher energy round your body. They are preparing you to switch on your full divine potential – your spiritual and psychic gifts.

CHAPTER 16

The Chakras of Atlantis

Chakras are our very essence. They are wheels of vibrating light within the body, which bring wisdom and inner knowledge. They affect every aspect of our lives and awaken us to the wealth of spiritual, psychological and physical power that we have within us. To take full advantage of the energy that can be poured into you through the chakras, you need to strengthen and cleanse the subtle body energy on a daily basis. (See exercise at the end of the chapter.)

The Twelve Chakra System

As we know, in pure Atlantis there were twelve fully-operational main chakras, as follows:

1. Stellar gateway. Today, this is approximately twelve inches (30 cm) above the top of the head.
2. Soul star. Today, this is approximately six inches (15 cm) above the top of the head.
3. Causal chakra. Today, this is located three to four inches (8–10 cm) behind the centre back of the head.
4. Crown chakra. This is at the top of the head.
5. Third eye chakra. This lies between the eyes, in the centre of the forehead.
6. Throat chakra. This is in the throat.

The Twelve Chakras

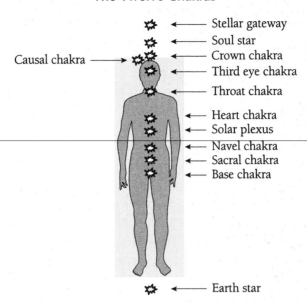

Stellar gateway

Soul star

Causal chakra

Crown chakra

Third eye chakra

Throat chakra

Heart chakra

Solar plexus

Navel chakra

Sacral chakra

Base chakra

Earth star

7. Heart chakra. This is found low down in the centre of the chest.

8. Solar plexus. This is in the solar plexus.

9. Navel chakra. This is just below the navel.

10. Sacral chakra. This is located in the lower abdomen.

11. Base chakra. This is at the base of the spine.

12. Earth star. This lies six inches (15 cm) below the feet.

STELLAR GATEWAY

In the golden years of Atlantis, the stellar gateway chakra was open in everyone, enabling them to access Source. This access was one of the first things that was lost when the ego began to manifest itself. At the time when it was fully in operation, they had greatly expanded skulls and brains. This chakra was quite near to the back of the head, but never touched it. Now it is approximately twelve inches (30 cm) above the head, but it has always remained outside the body. It can never belong to one thing for it is all things at the same time.

It is through the activation of this chakra that highly spiritual humans will experience ultimate consciousness. In current times, only a very few people – those who have lived in seclusion in a sacred place and have devoted their lives to spirit – can activate the stellar gateway. However, higher energies are now being beamed to Earth and people are waking up to their spiritual potential very quickly, so more people will make the connection. Only when this chakra is active can humans truly comprehend their oneness with Source. For this to happen, our minds and hearts must be able to detach from everything associated with personality and ego and our soul needs to be open.

The knowing of oneness is inbuilt into us, as is the vision of walking, which spurs a baby to totter and fall many times before he can balance and move forward on his own two feet. Occasionally, people have tried to access the stellar gateway through hallucinogenic drugs, but such attempts fry the brain and prevent any further spiritual progress in that life. Some people have unconsciously tried to make the connection without being spiritually, emotionally, mentally or physically ready and have damaged their neural pathways, resulting in illnesses such as schizophrenia and manic depression.

But it is now time for people who are spiritually worthy and sensibly grounded to move on to an ascension pathway, which will open their stellar gateway and enable them to bring back the purity and incredible spiritual grace of the Golden Age. Remember, the energy of Atlantis is returning. The time is NOW.

SOUL STAR
The soul star is the link between the stellar gateway and the causal and crown chakras. Its purpose is to take the pure energy of the

stellar gateway and filter it into the soul level of spiritually-attuned humans of today.

The soul enters the soul star when it leaves the physical body at death. Here the soul begins to learn about its oneness with all things and only when it 'knows' this can it move forward to the next stage. The soul star has the unique ability to assimilate light, but if this chakra is to be activated then it is essential that the Earth chakra is also working. They are two halves of one whole and must be in balance.

The soul star is the eleventh chakra, and number 11 signifies a new start. It represents the potential we have to reinvent our lives – of course, this is how the Atlanteans lived in the golden era. In current times the soul star is above the head, but formerly it was located within the brain structure.

When we are capable of knowing that all things share the same space – the same spiritual essence – unconditional love will return to humanity. Then our balanced yin and yang, the masculine and feminine within ourselves, will radiate into the world and close the widening gaps of separateness between us. It is time to listen to our hearts and our souls for we can never know from our intellect.

All the knowledge in the world is not equal to love.

In order to open the soul star we must work to neutralise mental pollution in the area of the eleventh chakra. Our discordant thoughts and beliefs, and those of our ancestors, have crystallised and these need to be swept away.

To do this:

1. Ground yourself. Black tourmaline placed on the floor at your feet will ground you.
2. Visualise a golden-white ball of energy radiating at the soul star chakra.

Remember that every time you have an unhealthy thought, projection or image you taint the area again, so this exercise will need to be continuously practised. Other things that pollute this area are drugs, depression and lower astral travel, as in dreams or angry imaginings.

When you do finally activate the soul star you will experience a profound connection to all things. The crystal selenite can help you with this.

Together, the stellar gateway and the soul star enable a merging of spiritual and earthly energies. The stellar gateway allows pure divine essence through from above, while the soul star draws up the kundalini and the animal instincts from Earth. These energies mix to become what we know as higher consciousness: our Godselves.

CAUSAL CHAKRA

This chakra is able to filter the soul force into the mental body, providing we are able to detach ourselves sufficiently from learned beliefs. This means we have to open our right brain and learn to see the whole picture and to seek expanded concepts. In order for the soul star to be able to transmit cosmic frequencies, the mind needs to be open. During Atlantean times, this chakra was encased within the inhabitants' more advanced brain structure.

It is through the causal chakra that we receive messages, or the downloading of concepts, from the higher spiritual realms. And it is only when mastery of the mind has been established that this chakra can be opened. Peace of mind and mental silence are essential and it can take years of meditation before people are ready for the causal chakra to fulfil its true purpose. It is when these conditions are met that you can begin to receive stellar transmissions into your thinking.

If you use blue kyanite while you meditate, it will bring you peace and stillness. This will enable you to be calm amid chaos, so that you can rise above all the trials and tribulations of earthly life and remain serene. Remember that ideas are like seeds planted in the ground: they take time to germinate and appear above the ground. Ideas gestate in the causal chakra and need time to manifest.

The lower chakras distribute information from the causal chakra into the rest of the body.

CROWN CHAKRA

This chakra, symbolised by the thousand-petalled lotus at the top of the head, opens up to accept light from the soul. Archangel Jophiel is in charge of the development of this chakra.

THIRD EYE CHAKRA

This chakra, in the centre of the forehead, is the centre of clair-voyance, divine wisdom and higher mental healing. It is looked after by Archangel Raphael.

THROAT CHAKRA

Archangel Michael rules this chakra. It is through it that we express our truth. When we resist our divine path, the back of the neck tenses up. That is the back of the throat chakra. When this centre is properly evolved we become powerful co-creators.

HEART CHAKRA

This chakra opens as we develop empathy, sympathy, compassion and unconditional love.

SOLAR PLEXUS

This is the centre of knowledge and most people hold fear here. As it evolves, it becomes golden with wisdom. We become tran-quil, serene and deeply peaceful as we access, again, the wisdom of our past lives.

NAVEL CHAKRA
This is the seat of emotions, sensuality and sociability.

SACRAL CHAKRA
Here, all sexual drives and feelings are held.

BASE CHAKRA
This chakra seeks to meet our basic survival needs of shelter, food and safety.

THE EARTH STAR
The Earth star and the two secondary chakras on the soles of the feet form a triangle pointing downwards. This triangle channels the divine essence through the physical body and into the ground itself, thereby creating our oneness with the Earth.

The physical plane is determined by the balance of opposites: 'As above, so below.' This means that the stellar gateway, the soul star and the causal chakra, in other words the highest chakras, can only fully express their light when the Earth star is awake. This means that we have to activate the Earth star at the same time as the three upper chakras. Remember that the Earth star can only be stimulated by the cosmic rays emanating from the three transpersonal chakras, so it cannot be opened in isolation. And the consciousness of the higher energy longs to find its ultimate fulfilment in harvesting the seeds of life rooted in the elements of matter. The balance created by the triangle of the three higher chakras and the Earth star allows the holy presence of the eternal force to renew the earth and to help heal it from the damage inflicted by humans.

When enough people carry this higher energy, the power of the pyramids will be renewed. Currently their energy is drained, as they are no longer directly linked to the emanations of the star systems to which they were originally fine tuned. This mis-alignment happened due to the shift of the Earth on its axis since the building of the pyramids. However, the raising of the consciousness of humanity will re-energise them.

When the Earth star chakras function at full capacity, the integration of spirit into matter will once more take place. This means that what humanity has destroyed can be replenished and Earth will be able to heal itself. It also means that we humans will be able to heal ourselves completely and live as they did in Atlantis. Currently, fear of the unknown is all that holds us back. The Sphinx, in Egypt, is here as a reminder that our animal nature, when it is governed by higher consciousness, can elevate us to divine consciousness. We are now asked to learn to live in accordance with the principles of harmony and unconditional love that governs the way of the Divine.

Secondary Chakras

There are also secondary chakras at the palm of each hand, the shoulders, elbows, knees and the soles of the feet – all of which can be used to focus spiritual energy. Healing energy flows through the palm chakras when someone is giving hands-on healing. To many people, the first indication that they are opening up as channels for healing is when they feel compassion for someone and their hands become warm or tingly. The energy is beginning to flow through their heart centres.

The shoulder chakras are connected to the heart, the energy of which flows through this point. They are also connected directly to the soles of the feet. When a healer lays hands on the recipient's shoulder, the feet chakra automatically open, which helps to ground the person who is receiving spiritual healing. This enables the light to flow through the entire system.

The knee chakra is a link because there is a long way between Earth and the base chakra. In the same way, the elbows act as a link between the shoulders and hands. The chakras under the soles of our feet are our connection to Earth. In Atlantis, the people walked miles each day, often in bare feet, which kept their contact with Earth strong. Even in the last 2,000 years monks would walk for three miles each day to keep themselves grounded so that they could safely allow their spirits to fly.

Tones and Frequencies

Each gateway has its own frequency and tone which aligns to our current musical scale:

* The stellar gateway is sixth-dimensional; its tone is top Do + 3.
* The causal chakra is fifth-dimensional; its tone is top Do + 2.
* The soul star is fourth-dimensional; its tone is top Do + 1.
* The crown chakra's tone is top Do.
* The third eye's tone is Ti.
* The throat chakra's tone is La.
* The heart chakra's tone is So.
* The solar plexus chakra's tone is Fa.
* The navel chakra's tone is Mi.
* The sacral chakra's tone is Re.
* The base chakra's tone is Do.
* The earth star's tone is bottom Do – 1.

Colours

Each chakra has a corresponding colour, that changes as the chakra rises in frequency. For most people who wish to bring back the energy of the twelve chakras it is appropriate to use the colours given below.

Stellar gateway – Gold. The energy of gold represents completion. We have made our journey and earned our place at the pinnacle. Our spiritual achievements, earned through many lifetimes, are recognised.

Soul star – Magenta. The colour magenta indicates an intense spiritual awareness, balanced by a connectedness to the ground. It is the colour of the divine feminine: earthly wisdom combined with spiritual knowledge.

Causal chakra – White. This is the colour of purity, clarity and perfection. It represents illumination, brings the qualities of all-knowing and all-seeing and allows us to open to higher wisdom.

Crown chakra – Violet. The high spiritual frequency of violet indicates devotion to spirit.

Third eye – Indigo. This deep blue holds the powers of mental healing and higher psychic development.

Throat chakra – Turquoise. This is the colour of expressing what you truly feel; speaking your truth.

Heart chakra – Green. The colour of nature, which represents balance and harmony.

Solar plexus – Yellow. This is the mind colour, which enables clarity of thought.

Navel chakra – Orange. A mixture of red and yellow, this colour indicates sociability and friendliness as well as emotional harmony.

Sacral chakra – Delicate pink. This is the colour of tenderness, which represents the spirit of sexuality – not the grosser feelings of desire or lust. It soothes and calms, encouraging feelings of love and nurturing. It takes the heat out of sexual encounters and returns the beauty and joy to the sexual expression of love.

Base chakra – Red. This gives us the energy to get our survival needs met.

Earth star – Black. This colour represents revival and renewal, and holds the potential of what we can be. Black encourages us to be still; to wait with trust in that stillness for our rebirth. It is the place where all earthly new beginnings await us.

EXERCISE: *Cleansing and Strengthening the Chakras*
Close your eyes and concentrate on slowing your breathing. Visualise all of the chakras in turn. Are they clean or dirty? Perhaps they are not rotating? Work to clean each chakra until you can see them as radiantly coloured discs, or beautiful flowers. Once they are all clean, they will be able to turn at their proper speed; whatever speed is comfortable and right for you. Once you have reached the stellar gateway see all twelve chakras as radiant and vibrating their power and energy through every cell of your body. Drink in this energy until you are ready to open your eyes. Doing this exercise regularly will help to keep your mind, body and spirit balanced.

The following exercises were used in the days of Atlantis by the High Priests and Priestesses, as well as by some specially selected Initiates. At sunrise and sunset each day, they would meditate to connect with the power of the sun as well as to align and ener-gise the twelve chakras. These exercises are powerful and must not be undertaken lightly.

This first exercise will particularly help to active the upper three transpersonal chakras.

EXERCISE: *Twelve-Chakra Breath*
You are now going to take one long breath up through all twelve chakras, resulting in a rainbow of twelve colours cascading out from the top of the stellar gateway. Working with each chakra in turn, visualise the Earth chakra, see the energy move from the Earth chakra to the base chakra, up to the sacral chakra and so on.

1. 10 minutes before sunrise or sunset, stand barefoot, ideally outside so your feet are on the earth, and face the sun. Place a hematite or black tourmaline crystal on the ground at your feet.

2. Close your eyes and take a deep breath, simultaneously raising your arms so that your palms face the sun. Keeping your arms straight, become aware of the warmth of the sun on the palms of your hands and at your third eye.

3. Take your attention to the Earth star, six inches (15 cm) below your feet.

4. Breathe in deeply and visualise drawing a band of energy from the Earth star, represented by the colour black, into your feet and up through your legs and into the base chakra.

5. Still breathing in, work up through the chakras, visualising the colour of each and adding all the colours to the energy rainbow at your base chakra:
   * Base – red
   * Sacral – delicate pink
   * Navel – orange
   * Solar plexus – yellow
   * Heart – green
   * Throat – turquoise
   * Third eye – indigo
   * Crown – violet
   * Causal – white
   * Soul star – magenta
   * Stellar gateway – gold

6. As the rainbow of energy erupts from the top of the stellar gateway, start to breathe out, and see the rainbow cascade down and around you, surrounding you in a bubble of pure vibrant energy. The energy then re-enters the earth near your feet and begins its journey back up through the twelve chakras, starting with the Earth star.

7. Continue this circular breath as the energy of the Earth star

makes contact with the transpersonal chakras. Keep this going, with your eyes closed, until the sun has set or just before it rises.

8. Then lower your arms, open your eyes and let your aura and body take in the energy of the rainbow while you enjoy the rising or setting of the sun.

DO NOT attempt the next section of this exercise until you can perform the first section without undue effort or strain.

EXERCISE: *Sun Connection*
Next comes the sun ritual that was performed daily by the Atlantean High Priests and Priestesses.

During the short period before the sun fully sets or rises, you may be able to look towards it with your peripheral vision. Never look directly at the sun, and if you feel any discomfort even while looking at it indirectly, close your eyes and rest them for a few minutes before looking again.

Don't worry if you can't look indirectly at the sun for more than thirty seconds – this will still be effective. Never stare directly at the sun in the three to five minutes before it rises or sets, as it could cause serious damage to the eyes.

1. Once you have established the twelve-chakra breath, open your eyes and hold the sun in your third eye.
2. When you hold the sun in your third eye, a powerful connection is made. It is important to continue the twelve-chakra breathing so that the Earth star and the stellar gateway are able to balance and come into alignment with one another. These two powerful energies coming together may cause several changes in what you feel:
   • You may feel the magnetic connection of the Earth with the sun.

- Once you can practise this exercise with expertise, you will be aware of the sun connecting with other planets in the galaxy.
- You can access previous experiences on other planets.
- If complete silence is maintained, it is possible for the consciousness to leave the body and become one with Source.

3. As the sun sinks or rises, continue the twelve-chakra breathing and be fully aware of your physical body. Bring the palms of your hands together at the middle of your chest, take a long, deep breath and reconnect with your immediate environment.

4. Sense the grounding energy of the Earth rising up through your hematite or black tourmaline crystal. Feel it rising all the way up the back of your body, from your feet and legs, up the spine and to the head, and then down the front of the body, into the legs, feet, and back into the Earth through the crystal. Feel the energy circulating until you are grounded again.

You can practice this meditation every day if you can feel the powerful energies of the Earth star and the stellar gateway aligning, and that you can handle and properly ground your spiritual energy. Otherwise, just continue to perform the twelve-chakra breath exercise regularly to clear and align your twelve-chakra system.

CHAPTER 17

The Psychic Arts

In the golden days of Atlantis, psychic gifts were highly regarded. They were never taken for granted and all latent abilities were honoured, valued and developed. Everyone was psychic to some degree, but not everyone had the full range of abilities. For instance, one person would be more clairvoyant, while another might be extremely clairaudient or highly telepathic. The trained priests had all of the gifts to an extraordinary level.

We include, in this chapter, exercises that were practised in Atlantis to develop psychic energies.

Clairvoyance

At the beginning, all the people were living at a fifth-dimensional frequency and therefore their third eyes were fully open. The third eye is a spiritual energy vortex, or chakra, found between the physical eyes in the centre of the forehead. It is the inner eye – rather like a crystal ball – with which clairvoyants can see the worlds beyond the veil of material illusion.

Atlanteans could see the elemental kingdom, fairies, elves, gnomes, salamanders, mermaids and many others, as well as the spirits of those who had passed over. Most significantly, they were able to access the spiritual realms and be aware of angels, unicorns and other spiritual beings. They could also receive guidance from these higher beings through vivid moving scenes impressed on their third eye.

In addition, they could communicate with each other by sending pictures. It was like being able to send an e-mail with a picture in it from mind to mind. For example, if a lady was talking telepathically to another person in Atlantis about a beautiful waterfall she had recently visited, the friend might want to see it. The first lady would be able to show it to her clairvoyantly, and these psychic pictures would be vivid and clear.

In our current times, when the frequency is lower, most clairvoyants receive information that is fragmented. We still place pictures into other people's minds, but it is usually done unconsciously.

Clairaudience

In the Golden Age, those who were predominantly clairaudient could hear streams of audible sentences offering guidance. Angels and higher beings were able to communicate directly with them. But the voices did not come only from disembodied beings. If a mother was separated from her child, she could tune into him or her. Then she would be able to hear what the child was saying to her over a distance. If someone wanted to communicate directions to a friend, they would link into the friend and guide him from several miles away.

In current, low-frequency times the 'telephone lines' of clairaudience tend to crackle, so most clairaudient people receive broken words or incomplete sentences. But even today many people have been surprised by hearing audible words – especially warnings from an invisible presence. Someone we know was staying in a tented camp in Africa. She was just about to get out of bed to go to the toilet, when a loud, commanding voice said, 'Don't get out of bed.' There was no one there, but the force of the disembodied voice was so powerful that she lay under the covers for the remainder of the night, not daring to move. She still wonders if there was a snake or poisonous spider lurking, which might have bitten her, but she is in no doubt that a higher being – possibly her guardian angel – saved her life.

Again and again, people have told us their stories of hearing angels singing over them in the night, especially at times of sorrow or great need. The beautiful thing about this is that angels often sing over our beds while we are asleep and very few of us hear them. Nevertheless, the vibration of love, peace and healing is showered over us.

There are still some gifted clairaudients living today. Diana was in Australia, being given a lift by a new acquaintance. They were travelling into a town which neither had visited before, and needed to park. The woman said, 'I'll ask my guide to direct us. Ah- He says we turn left at the traffic lights, travel for 200 yards, turn right at a roundabout, and left at the next turning into a car park. There will be a parking place prepared for us in the third row at the far end.' And so it was! Everyone was clairaudient in this way in Atlantis.

Clairsentience

This is the ability to sense another person's pain or physical feelings in your own body. If you can feel the hairs on your body stand up when you enter a frightening place, you are sensing the atmosphere of a place. If you understand something by 'feeling it in your waters' or 'knowing it in your bones', this is clairsentience. If your body tenses up when you meet a certain person, your senses are warning you to be careful. The sacral is the chakra of clairsentience.

Many people today are clairsentient without realising it. You may sense when the weather is going to change by getting a headache. You may know if your child is doing really well in a test because you feel relaxed in your body. A woman woke one night feeling sick and terribly ill. Her husband came in late and said everything was fine. The sickness went, but a feeling of anxiety remained and she discovered later that she had woken feeling ill at the moment he was with another woman. Another lady had a persistent nagging backache, which she associated with her elderly mother, but could not understand what it meant. Then the phone rang to tell her that her mother had fallen and had been taken into hospital. The backache then disappeared.

The organs of the body are like antennae, which sense danger. Sensitive people often pick up disasters taking place at the other end of the world by a feeling of tension in different organs of their body. Often they do not know what is going to happen but they feel the danger through the 'antennae' of their bodies. As soon as they see on the news that the violence or outrage has already taken place, the tension dissolves.

The physical body is a barometer of the world around you. If you stay conscious of the messages it gives you, you can learn a great deal. Unfortunately, we often receive mixed messages, especially when we are children. Our body tells us something is wrong and our parents tell us everything is okay, when it is not. This causes confusion, until we no longer trust our intuition. The greatest gift we can give our family, friends and colleagues is to be honest and congruent. When we are unconscious of the messages of our body, illness can creep up unnoticed, relationships can collapse without us being aware and we fail to read the signposts of our lives. When we start to notice and become conscious of our bodies, our intuition and psychic awareness opens up like a flower. In early Atlantis, this ability was sharply honed because they were conscious, congruent beings.

Seeing Auras

Every living thing radiates an aura, or electromagnetic energy field, in which everything is depicted: your history, your deepest thoughts, your fears, hopes and current feelings. When a true psychic tunes into your aura, you stand naked, for all is revealed in vibrant technicolour. In these days most people get a sense of a person, but very few retain the ability of seeing all.

As soon as we feel shame, we try to keep something secret. Immediately, we close our hearts for fear of being found out and judged. In those glorious days of honesty and acceptance, there was no judgement. All hearts were open. When your heart is open and radiating love, beautiful fingers of pink light spill from it, reaching out to touch and enfold everyone and everything around you. In pure Atlantis, when everyone could see the radiant colours of the energy fields around others, nothing could be hidden, so there were no secrets. All people were open, honest and truthful.

Psychometry

Every object is imbued with the energy of its owner. At this time of Atlantis, if someone found, for example, a child's toy, the finder would pick it up and know instantly where and to whom it should be returned. These days psychometry is used to divine information about the past, very often about the life of the person who has presented the object.

Remote Viewing

Remote viewing is a mental faculty that allows a person to give details about a target that, due to distance, time or shielding, is inaccessible to normal senses. The mind is capable of witnessing any event, thing or being in the cosmos. It enables you accurately to experience, sense, feel, taste, smell, hear, and minutely describe any event, person, being, place or object that has ever existed, does exist or will exist. In theory, there is nothing that cannot be remotely viewed. Once you are able to remote view spiritual beings like the Christ or the Buddha, you are never quite the same again.

Remote viewing may seem to be the same as clairvoyance and other forms of psychic discipline, but there are two things that make it unique. The first is that remote viewing usually involves all the senses, so not only do you see a picture, but you can taste, smell, hear and touch it as well. When people are being viewed, you can sense their thoughts and feel their feelings. The second difference is that remote viewing can be accompanied by an out-of-body experience and is often referred to as bi-location. This means that part of your awareness is where you currently are, and part of your awareness is at the event being viewed.

Practising remote viewing can heighten your awareness of your subtle senses and intuition. It can also be used for personal and spiritual growth. Developing remote-viewing skills is easy. However, it takes time and you must follow a step-by-step process. This is a very deep and involved subject, too much to cover in this book, but we have given a simple exercise at the end of this chapter for those who are interested. For those who wish to access more in-depth knowledge of remote viewing, the internet offers a great deal of information.

The applications for remote viewing are almost limitless, but the Atlantean priesthood used it for:

Evaluation. It enabled them to weigh up various alternatives about when and where to build new temples, healing chambers or homes. Using skills like astrology, numerology and geomancy they would already have fixed upon a specific site and time when the building could be started. To ensure there were no unforeseen factors to be taken into account, the Atlanteans would remote view the completed building at points in the future. It also enabled them to assess accurately what technology they could next introduce.

Location. It enabled them to find mineral deposits or missing people. (This skill is still used by the police. For example, in 1974 the Berkeley Police Department in San Francisco contacted the Stanford Research Institute and asked that their people with remote-viewing abilities help in tracing the kidnapped heiress Patricia Hearst.)

Diagnosis. They would use it to scan the body for medical problems, or to pinpoint mechanical problems, and health, safety and environmental hazards.

Forecasting. Earthquakes, volcanic activity, political conditions and technological developments were all forecast by this means.

One reason the Atlanteans were able to maintain their state of equanimity for so long was because their ability to see the future through remote viewing enabled them to prevent potential problems and instead create something positive. This meant there was nothing to fear.

Healing

Psychic healing and many other kinds of healing were used in Atlantis and we discuss this in Chapter 23.

Psychic Development

When we humans live away from nature, our hearts become hard. A lack of respect for growing, living things soon leads to a lack of respect for animals and other people. The Atlanteans loved nature and through their constant interaction with it, their ordinary senses were developed to a very high degree. Because of this they were able to make use of other inner senses and this extended their range of conscious awareness, making them more psychic.

Those of us who live in large communities, big towns and cities today are not so close to the natural world and, as a consequence, our normal perceptions and perceived capabilities are not adequately exercised and developed. This means that we only use a comparatively small part of our sensory equipment.

Atlanteans knew that when they fine-tuned their ordinary senses, it resulted in an expansion of awareness. This gave them what we now call extrasensory perception, a highly-developed sixth sense. In order to awaken the sixth or psychic sense, we first need to awaken the five senses of touch, taste, smell, sight and hearing. Making better use of the ordinary senses is the first step to awakening the inner psychic senses. And this is something we can all practise.

EXERCISE: *Awakening Your Senses*
1. Take yourself to a peaceful place in nature, among the trees. This might be on a hillside or near a river or stream. Even in our modern cities there should be a park where you can be surrounded by some natural beauty.
2. Find a tree that has space around it, and a good-sized trunk. Sit facing the direction of the sun, with your back against the tree trunk so that you can sit upright in comfort with the trunk of the tree supporting your back.
3. Now spend a few minutes concentrating on each of your senses in turn:

Sight. Watch the sunlight dance on the leaves of the trees; notice the rich shades of the colours of the leaves. Explore the colours of flowers and shrubs, and the crinkly pattern of the leaves. In winter, examine the texture of the tree trunks and the arms and fingers of the branches. Watch the clouds as they move across the sky. Consider the weaving of the grass near your feet. Watch the movement of any animals, birds or insects that are around you. Just put all your attention into looking and seeing.

Hearing. Now switch all your attention to listening. Just listen for and to the sounds of nature. Hear the whisper of the wind in the trees, the songs of the birds, the rustle of small moving creatures, the hum of insects.

Touch. Concentrate on the sense of touch. Feel the warmth of the sun on your face, the caress of the wind in your hair, or the kiss of rain on your lips. Take off your shoes and let your feet sink into the soft, springy turf beneath you. Feel your oneness with nature.

Smell. Smell the scent of the grass, the sweet fragrance of flowers, the earthiness of the soil beneath your feet. Put all your attention into your sense of smell and breathe in the fragrance of nature.

Taste. The senses of smell and taste are linked. For each perfume in the air, open your mouth and allow your tongue to discover the taste of it. It may start the saliva flowing as your taste buds respond to the freshness.

If you spend at least five minutes putting each of your senses to work in this way, you will experience a contact with nature that you have possibly never known. Even if you only spend half an hour each week in this tranquillity, within a few weeks you will recognise an opening of your senses, a sharpening of your intuition and creativity, and an awareness of the spirit of things. One day, when you perform this exercise, you will become aware of the sounds behind those of the Earth; the hidden sounds of nature. This is what the Atlanteans were able to access.

EXERCISE: *Psychometry*

Obtain something – preferably made of metal or wood – that a person carries with them for much of the time. This could be a watch, any piece of jewellery or even a set of keys. We always like to ensure that the person whose possession is being read knows its history, since when you are practising psychometry you are opening yourself up to the energies contained in the object.

Enclose the item in your hands, close your eyes, and relax yourself by taking three deep breaths. Keep your eyes closed and move the object around in your hands. Shaaron likes to move it around so that she gets in touch with all its surfaces. You may find it works better for you to keep it still. This is a very personal experience so accept whatever works best for you.

Simply share with the owner whatever images, words or sensations come to you. A lady once gave Shaaron her watch, and she immediately saw a Christmas scene with a large roaring fire in the fireplace, two young girls, a vicar and a dog. She described the scene and its characters in detail, and the lady told Shaaron that she was seeing her and her twin sister, their father and their dog from a Christmas many years before.

This skill improves significantly the more you use it.

EXERCISE: *Reading Auras*

The easiest auras to see are those of trees on a bright sunny day.

Relax, then look at a tree with half-closed eyes. You may see a band of white light round it, and sometimes this light will have silver sparks moving round in it.

Hills and mountains also radiate a high vital force, which is often easy to see. If you do not see anything the first few times, persist. Remember to relax into it and not to try too hard.

You can also practise reading the auras of your friends, an exercise that is fun and also develops your psychic abilities. It can be practised with one person, but it is even better in a group. Do not necessarily expect to *see* anything. You can read auras with all your senses.

1. Make sure the light is bright.
2. Ask one person to sit with his or her back to a plain wall.

3. As you look at the person, say the first thing that comes to you. You may have a flash of colour, or a sense of a past life, or a feeling of contentment. You may be aware of their spirit guide or a knowing about something. The only thing that stops you participating in this is your fear of failure, which comes from ego.

EXERCISE: *Remote Viewing*

To do a simple remote-viewing exercise you need four people: the controller, two observers and the viewer. The reasons for the controls and checks is that it is easy to pass information on telepathically, rather than by remote viewing.

The controller selects pictures or images that will be the 'targets' – the objects the viewer will describe. These images should be different from each other and quite specific. For example, a row of shops would not be a good subject because of their similarities. However, Buckingham Palace or any unique-looking building would be ideal. Only the controller may know what the images are. Each image is then sealed in an opaque envelope (and it is a good idea to place this envelope inside a second envelope). Each envelope is given a unique number.

On a specified date, one of the observers will select one of the envelopes at random and take it somewhere away from the viewer. It could be the next room, a different town or even another country. At a prearranged time he will open the envelope and look at the picture or target for a previously-agreed length of time.

The viewer needs a pen and note pad, or even a tape recorder, and should be in a place that is free from as much external distraction as possible. It has been discovered that a low light is helpful. It is also helpful to take time to relax and clear the mind, so as to be open and receptive. The second observer will be in the same room as the viewer.

At the prearranged time, the viewer focuses on the target and either speaks, notes or draws his impressions. If he is experiencing difficulties, the observer with him may assist by asking questions. As he has no idea what the picture is, these may be specific – yet general. For example, what colours do you see? What sounds do you hear?

Let's assume that the first observer is looking at a picture of the Blackpool Tower. If the viewer has already said, for instance, 'I see a tall metal structure,' then questions might be: Is the structure outside? Is it a solid structure? How does the structure make you feel?

When the specified time is up, the first observer replaces the target in the envelope, notes on it the date and time it is sealed. He returns to the viewer's location and hands over the envelope to the controller. The four people meet together so that the viewer can receive feedback – this is a very important step as it reinforces the viewer's skill.

A note here on what you can expect from the viewer. Using the example of Blackpool Tower, what the viewer may tell you or draw for you could be rudimentary fragments – remember this is a skill you are developing – for instance you may see sketches like the ones below. The viewer may use words like 'tall metal structure', 'struts', or 'tower'. When asked about his feelings regarding what he sees, he may come up with words like 'fun', 'excitement' or 'fear', if he is afraid of heights. If you ask him what he can smell,

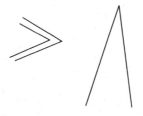

Example of Early Impressions

hear or see, then he may say 'lights', 'music', 'fried onions', 'candyfloss', 'sweet, sickly smell' or 'the sea'. It would very unlikely, at this early stage, that he could tell you it was Blackpool Tower. However, once the skill had been fully developed, with regular and consistent practice, it would be possible to name targets that you recognised.

CHAPTER 18

The Power of the Mind in Atlantis

From the earliest age, the children were taught about the power of the mind. Your thoughts are like soldiers. Individually they cannot do too much damage or achieve a great deal. But together they form an army commanded by your mind. When you give orders to disciplined, trained soldiers they can accomplish great things. In the same way, when your thoughts are directed properly and focused on the desired outcome, the mind becomes an incisive tool with which to create. This is only possible when the commands are clear and working in alignment with each other. Of course, if you are in charge of an unruly rabble, they will run rings round you. Similarly, if your thoughts are all over the place, your mind controls you. Contradictory thoughts create inner conflict, which is mirrored in your outer life. The Atlanteans were taught that a quiet, still mind is a healthy one. A whirling, overcrowded one is sick. And it is only through a serene and ordered mind that the angelic forces and Illumined Masters can communicate. That is why the people of Golden Atlantis spent silent, meditative time in nature or listening to appropriate music whenever they could.

Channelling

When you still your mind and raise your frequency to bring in information from the higher spiritual beings, you are channelling.

The High Priests and Priestesses, of course, were the only members of the priesthood to channel information and guidance from the Intergalactic Council. However, this was a skill that was taught and used by all priests from the time they became Novices. The populace did not develop these skills. Now, however, many lightworkers – who are reincarnated priests – are remembering the wonders of drawing down information in this way, because they are recalling their ancient gifts. It is time now to quieten your mind and reconnect with the forces of light and love.

You may have been channelling without being aware of it. For many people it comes as flashes of inspiration or flowing creativity. Everyone can practise communicating with their guides, but you need to raise your frequency higher in order to connect with the angels and Illumined Ones. It is important to remember that higher beings will only speak to you with love, inspiration and compassion. Your intention is very important and left-brain focus and concentration need to be balanced with right-brain creativity, intuition and openness.

If you are very familiar with your angel, guides or masters, you may not sense very much because you are already used to their vibration. On the other hand, you may feel hot or expanded, or you may sense colour, perfume, music or lights. Sometimes when people are channelling they receive clairvoyant pictures. Others receive a telepathic download or stream of consciousness, which may seem like their own thoughts. However, actual channelled information has a clarity, purity and spontaneity that sets it apart, and brings with it a knowing that the guidance is from a higher source. When you have connected with the higher forces in this way you will carry more light.

Divination

The art of looking into the future was rarely practised in Golden Atlantis, for they realised that the thoughts, words and actions of the 'now' inevitably create the future. When the purity of Atlantis started to corrupt, the priests encouraged divination as a means of disempowering fearful souls seeking reassurance about what might happen. We can now use it in a positive way to gain clarity and confirmation about our future so that we can take higher decisions about our direction.

Tarot

In current times, the Tarot is often used as a focus for forecasting the future and as such can be very effective. In Atlantis, however, it was developed purely as a tool for spiritual guidance. Families would have tarot cards and, because the energy was lighter, they were used to gain insights and greater perspectives. Together they would ask a question. Each member of the family would choose a card to enable him or her to understand their role in the project, as well as their contribution to it. From this they would develop their goals and make a treasure map, as discussed later in the book.

Telepathy

Telepathy is mind-to-mind thought transference. In the early times of Atlantis, people did not need to talk to each other, as they consciously practised telepathy. Most could only use telepathy over short distances, but those who were trained could communicate over miles.

When a child was away from home, the mother would telepathically contact the child to discover where it was. If she wanted to speak to her husband, who was away in the fields, for example, she would tune into his frequency and communicate with him.

Of course, in the Temples of Education, the priests imparted teachings telepathically, as this bypassed the critical censor of the conscious mind and allowed the cosmic information to slip into the deeper mind. While we would now consider this suspect, as it could influence someone against their will, in the pure times all teaching was done for the highest good and there was never a cause for concern.

INTERGALACTIC TELEPATHY

In the early golden days when the High Priests and Priestesses channelled information from the Intergalactic Council, it was like tuning into a radio signal. The guidance they received was loud and clear. The Alta and Magi also had telepathic links with the rulers of other planets, to exchange knowledge and information, and receive the benefit of their wisdom.

When Atlantis started to descend into corruption and chaos, however, there were constant problems to address. Then they needed to have frequent two-way conversations with the Intergalactic Council and they used telepathy. But because the frequency on the planet was becoming heavier, this method of communication used a great deal of energy and was very tiring. Indeed, before the fall, the twelve great rulers of Atlantis sometimes had to gather together – which boosted the energy – in order to have an accurate telepathic conversation with the Council.

Palmistry

The body is a hologram. Eyes, ears, feet, hands: every part of you contains information about the whole of you and your soul mission.

In hands, the non-dominant palm contains the blueprint of your life and what you are here to achieve in your lifetime. The dominant hand reflects what you have actually done, and therefore what you are likely to accomplish in the future. It tells you whether you are on course for your part in the divine plan. A skilled and spiritual palmist can guide you towards your divine destiny. In pure Atlantis, palmistry was a skill that was not really necessary as they had other gifts to provide them with similar information.

After the corruption of Atlantis, the black Magi tried to take over the rule of Atlantis. They had their own agenda, which was based on controlling the people and taking power. They needed to know if the people were following their predestined plan or were coming into line with the ambitions of the Magi. Then they used palmistry as a means of gauging that the flock were behind them.

Astrology and Numerology

These subjects are so significant that we devote a chapter to each of them.

EXERCISE: *Mind Expansion 1*
Today, we only use a small portion of our mind, so this is an exercise to expand our brain capacity. Do not give up easily. Be tenacious when you seek to expand your mind. Also be brave when you do this, for revelations tend to come in startling ways.

1. Obtain a tektite crystal and a piece of bright red material – ideally silk, but cotton will do.
2. Take your crystal and cloth to a quiet place – in nature, if possible.
3. Sit on the ground and place the tektite crystal in front of you, in the centre of your piece of red cloth.
4. Meditate or concentrate intensely on the crystal.
5. It will help if you set out a crystal in each of the four directions, as follows, for it is from these directions that expanded understandings will come to you.
   * North: Snow Quartz
   * South: Red Jasper
   * East: Yellow Jasper
   * West: Jet

Signs of opening up will sometimes appear to you as lights, then in the form of words or images. Sometimes a great deal of information is given. However, do not be disappointed if you do not receive anything immediately, as it can take time, often several attempts, before the veils are released. The more you do this exercise, the sooner you will open your mind to receive divine communication.

EXERCISE: *Mind Expansion 2 – 'Becoming'.*
This exercise is known as 'becoming' and was used in Atlantis by the first settlers. Today it is still used by Native American Indians. The purpose of this particular exercise is to 'become' something else and it helps to deepen your relationship with the rest of creation. It allows you to build harmony and inner peace.

It is best to use a faceted crystal for this exercise, as it helps you consider the various aspects of the subject that you are going to become.

Now go to a quiet place where you can be undisturbed. Choose something to work with. This can be a tree, plant, flower, rock or even a crystal. Where it is small, you need to be able to hold it in your hand. You may pick a flower, with its agreement, but do not uproot it. If you choose a tree then sit with both hands resting against the trunk. Whatever you select remember to ask for its permission before doing this exercise.

For this example we will use a rock.

1. Sit on the ground and hold the rock in the palms of your cupped hands. Do not squeeze it, just let it rest comfortably.
2. Focus your attention upon the rock.
3. Imagine, and know, that you are becoming the rock.
4. Feel its coolness, its firmness, its outer and inner texture, its durability and its life force.
5. Reflect on how some rocks have lasted forever.
6. Think about the ways in which rocks serve humans, and what humans have done with them.

7. Think about the ways in which the universe uses rocks, and what rocks have to teach us.
8. Open your mind to another kind of consciousness. For example, a rock is static, solid, patient, slow and timeless.
9. Sit like this for as long as you are comfortable. As you may have slipped into the consciousness of the rock, before you stand up allow some time to ground yourself by taking three deep, long breaths. If you still feel slightly dizzy when you stand, then stamp your feet on the ground several times.

EXERCISE: *Develop Your Psychic Ability*
For best results, please ensure that you first do the 'Awakening Your Senses Exercise', at the end of Chapter 17.

Using fairly thick white cardboard, create a set of six cards using the symbols below. To aid the clarity of the images ensure that the symbols are in bold, dark blue against a white background and that you cannot see the symbols from the back of the card.

You will also need a notebook in which to keep a record of your progress, as this will help you to monitor your improvement. Write the numbers 1 to 21 down the left-hand side of your notebook.

Keep your practice sessions standard, i.e. make the same number of attempts each session. We recommend that you do this exercise a total of twenty-one times in each session.

These are the symbols:

1. Shuffle your six cards so that you cannot see the symbols.
2. Place the cards face down and side-by-side on a table in front of you.

3. Choose a card and place it in front of you. Do not look at the symbol.
4. Now gently concentrate your attention on the card.
5. Take the first symbol that appears to you. You may see it, hear it or simply sense it, depending on whether you are naturally clairvoyant, clairaudient or clairsentient.
6. Once you sense what the card is – remember to go with the initial first message – turn it over.
7. Each time you are correct put a tick on your list in your notebook.
8. Gather the cards together again, repeat steps 1 to 7 and work through them until you have done this twenty-one times.
9. At the end of the session total the number of ticks you have and make a note of it.

Do not be worried if your score is low initially. Remember that you are developing a new skill and will improve. Also, do not be concerned if for a while, you seem to get worse. The reason is that your mind often rebels against your efforts to change it. However, it invariably co-operates with you within quite a short period of time.

Once you have mastered these symbols you will find further symbols on our websites: www.dianacooper.com and www.shaaronhutton.co.uk. Use the same system to practise with these more challenging symbols.

EXERCISE: *Channelling*
Have paper and pen ready if you wish to write down what you receive. If you do not feel safe, warm and loved, open your eyes and come out of trance.

1. Decide what question you wish to ask. You may want to know what you are learning from a particular situation, or to receive insights about personal or world situations.

2. Ground yourself by visualising your feet on the floor and roots connecting you deep into the Earth.

3. Breathe deeply and quietly for a few minutes, relaxing your body and mind.

4. Visualise a stream of golden light flowing down into your crown and through your body.

5. See it form a cloak of golden light around you, protecting you.

6. Fill your mind with the colour of white gold.

7. When you are ready, ask your question. At this point you may feel a connection with a higher being.

8. If you wish to, ask who is working with you.

9. Relax as a stream of consciousness flows through you.

10. Thank the being who has given you information and close down.

11. Make notes if appropriate.

CHAPTER 19

Using and Changing Energy

Everything is energy, only the density varies. Some energy is so dense that it becomes a physical object, while elsewhere it is as light as air and therefore invisible to us. There are a number of ways in which humans can change the density and form of energy, until it becomes touchable.

As we know, every thought and emotion we send out starts to change energy and creates our lives, but in the third dimension this is a slow process.

Prayer

Prayer is a supplication for something. If you ask very clearly from a centred space and then detach from the results, your prayer will be answered – assuming that it is for the highest good. This spiritual law is activated by faith, and states, 'pray, believing, and it is already granted.' The universal energy also responds to prayers from an open heart that demonstrates compassion and love.

Materialisation

Materialisation is similar, except that you visualise and focus on your dream, affirming that it is already there. Again, you must detach from ego desire and rely on the angelic realms to bring it to you if it is for the highest good.

Imaging

Most of the people of early Atlantis used imaging to manifest objects from the invisible realms into the physical world. This very powerful tool could draw objects from the unmanifest world without the intercession of the angels. Because they were dedicated to controlling their minds, everyone could create very powerful thought forms. They were also taught from childhood to focus on the end not the means. So they imaged their desired result with concentrated focus. Imagination involves picturing or sensing something and is a building brick for manifesting. However, to image something is much more intense. It involves visualising every tiny detail so clearly that you can feel, sense, hear and taste it. Most important, you must then vividly experience the emotions of having whatever it is in your life.

Precipitation

Precipitation is a process of fashioning the apparently intangible pure energy into a physical object. The highly-trained Priests and Magi were able to manipulate energy in this way using sound, crystals and the power of their minds. They developed breath-taking powers.

Even today there are yogis who fashion energy into vibbhuti ash, which is sacred healing ash, or rings or other jewellery. Many people wear rings manifested by Sai Baba, an Indian guru, which appear seemingly from thin air. According to Kumeka, precipitation is simply a matter of belief that anything that is pure energy can be made dense.

Upon the seeding of Golden Atlantis, the High Priests, Priestesses and Magi started to form a pool of high-frequency energy. It took some generations for this pool to build up, and when it did the priests, shamans and people with special responsibility had access to it in its entirety. However, everyone could draw from it to some extent. It could be used to boost telepathy over a distance, for manifestation and precipitation, healing, the regeneration of limbs, soul retrieval or at any time when a surge of energy was needed.

In the very earliest days, the power of precipitation was not needed as the people built what they needed for their communal use with their hands. But as more generations incarnated and the population increased, they needed more and larger homes and temples. Their skill in the use of energy strengthened. A group of specialists from the priesthood was selected because of their abilities in mind control and precipitation. They were specifically trained and started to use these powers regularly, offering their services to the community. Drawing on the power of the Great Pool of Pure Energy, they could create homes and buildings, temples, roads, swimming pools, fountains and, later, transports that we would call hoverbuses. They also built space ships, which were made of materials that we have no knowledge of, and many other things.

The Great Pool is now being rebuilt by the Illumined Ones, together with healers and lightworkers who are in incarnation, and who are unconsciously adding their light to the communal energy source.

It is important to remember that the early Atlanteans were also incredibly talented engineers, architects, designers and builders, and preferred the satisfaction of using these more mundane skills. However, in order to assemble the materials they needed for building, they would use telekinesis, which is the ability to move objects. They especially gathered orichalcum, a locally found pink-gold-coloured metal, and natural materials such as stone, as well as other resources not of this planet.

Using telekinesis, they placed huge stones in the correct positions. Again, this involved being able to change the density of objects and lighten them with the power of the mind. It was a matter of knowing you could do it. Knowing is faith, which consists of love and oneness, and is the most powerful energy in the universe.

If they wanted to materialise, for example, a form of transport such as a flying craft, first the designer had to perceive it. In order to move the energy from pure and light to dense and tangible, every detail of it had to be imaged with intense clarity. We can only wonder at the thought process involved.

Remember, even the ordinary people of that time had infinitely greater cerebral faculty than we do now.

Everything that we discuss in this book is within our ability to achieve now, as long as we have the materials with which to work. Clearly, the extraterrestrial metals and crystals have long been withdrawn and are currently unavailable. Also, at present, with our limited brainpower, we could not precipitate something as complex as a car, because we do not possess the knowledge, the discipline or the clarity to hold the design in our minds. But we could precipitate something simple, like a plate, or make water boil in a cup by imaging the heat.

Telekinesis and Apportation

Telekinesis is the ability to dematerialise an object external to yourself and rematerialise it in a different place. In Atlantis this was considered to be an average and ordinary gift and was used by everyone to move things.

Crystals have the power to apport, in other words to dematerialise *themselves*, move to another location and rematerialise again. Diana had an experience of this many years ago when she organised a crystal workshop in her home. At the end of the weekend the facilitator asked her to choose a crystal as a present. She picked a beautiful clear quartz, a masculine crystal. The facilitator told her that she really needed a different one, which was a cloudy quartz, a feminine crystal. However, she decided she wanted to stay with her original choice, so he packed the rejected stone to take it home.

A few days later, Diana went into the shed in her garden, and there in the middle of the floor sat the cloudy quartz. She immediately phoned the facilitator to ask if he had left the crystal at her house, but he confirmed that he had not. He did say, however, that it had obviously come back to Diana on purpose and she must keep it.

Years later, Kumeka confirmed that the crystal had apported because those two crystals came in to work together. They were partners and that was their destiny. They would only ever go to a person who needed them together. Diana was offered any crystal in the room but in selecting one, she unconsciously chose both. The choice of the crystals to be a pair and the fact that Diana kept one of them was enough to create the energy for the other to apport back to its partner. Love is the glue of the universe. Diana still has that pair of crystals and always keeps them together.

Teleportation

Teleportation is the ability to move ourselves through time and space and rematerialise somewhere else. During teleportation the cellular structure of the body breaks down into an atomic energy stream, pure light that pours along the ley lines. The person rematerialises at the other end. This process overcomes gravity.

Levitation

True levitation, as practised in Atlantis, meant that you had to develop the power to control your energy fields so that your entire body could rise. Flying yogis, who practise certain meditation techniques, can partially do this by raising their kundalini energy, and this allows them to lift from the ground for a short time.

There is a simple form of levitation that everyone can try. One person sits in a chair while four people surround him. Each places a finger under the person. Yes – just one finger. Really try to lift the person and it will be impossible – unless you are some super person! When you are certain you cannot lift your friend, take your fingers away. Let all those who are standing step back for a moment to centre yourselves. Then each in turn place your right hands, one on top of the other, on his head. Follow with the left hands. Press very lightly, while holding a vision of your friend rising. Take your hands off his head and put the same finger under him, and lift.

Diana has participated in these levitations many times and has seen big men rising a couple of feet in the air, to their total astonishment. It does not always work but, interestingly, when it is going to, you know it will. Kumeka says that it is a matter of belief. If you believe it will work, it will. Some people, of course, believe unconsciously. Their energy will enable the person to rise. Others are consciously or unconsciously sceptical and this will ground the person. If you all believe, the person in the chair will always levitate.

Lucid Dreaming and Dream Chambers

Most dreams are messages from your unconscious or sub-conscious minds, which tell you about emotions that you have not dealt with. Others, from the superconscious, are about higher connections in the inner planes, and spiritual teachings.

Lucid dreaming is the ability to influence, consciously, the outcome of your dreams. This means that situations, objects, people and worlds can be created and transformed. We are just discovering the power of lucid dreaming, but for the Atlanteans it was a part of their everyday – or night – lives. Just as we currently practise visualisation as a tool to improve our lives, the Atlanteans used the soul energy of their dreams. They took control of the images and changed them to their desired outcome. This work in the inner planes manifests things into your physical reality and is, therefore, extremely powerful. It must be practised with the highest integrity.

The dream chamber would be used for goals that affected the whole community. An Initiate would lead a specially-selected group of individuals in a communal lucid dream.

The Tibetan Buddhist, Tarthang Tulku, in his book, *Openness Mind*, wrote, 'Dreams are a reservoir of knowledge and experience, yet they are often overlooked as a vehicle for exploring reality. In the dream state our bodies are at rest, yet we see and hear, move about, and are even able to learn. When we make good use of the dream state, it is almost as if our lives were doubled: instead of a hundred years, we live two hundred.'

It is now possible to teach a person the art of lucid dreaming and because of this it is rapidly becoming a tool for problem solving, self-healing and personal growth. Life in the world of lucid dreams is unbounded and the seemingly impossible can become possible.

TREASURE MAPS AND DREAM BOOKS
Another tool the Atlanteans used to enhance their lives was the treasure map. This was a fun and creative way of focusing on the manifestation of their goals. Treasure maps were created by individuals, families or whole communities. The usual goal-setting principles apply: define, focus and release. When they were clear about their aim, the family would get together and create a pictorial treasure map, which would be displayed on the sitting room wall. They would have fun drawing and painting representations of their goal. For instance, if they needed a larger place to live, they would create a very detailed picture (treasure map) of their desired home. It would include an accurate floor

plan, pictures of each of them enjoying their new abode, paintings of their pets, and pressed flowers from the garden – only taken with the permission of the flowers, of course. Also, they would include scenes of friends or family visiting, as well as other scenarios with them all celebrating their move and being happy there. In addition, the map would include affirmations related to their dream, and always the affirmation: 'This, or something better, now manifests for us for the highest good.'

Once they were happy with their treasure map they would hang it up where they would see it often. Then they would release the goal to the universe for it to manifest. In the days that followed, as each of them looked at their treasure map and remembered the fun they had making it, they were adding positive energy to the manifestation of their dream.

Today, when we make a treasure map we can use many ready-made things, for example: photographs, and we can still have enormous enjoyment using them. Finding the pictures can be a joy in itself. Indeed with today's technology we can find a suitable one in a magazine and change the people in it to reflect us. We could cut out a bride and groom from a journal and replace their faces with our own.

The Atlanteans were a very open and supportive people with no secrets from each other, but in our current society we sometimes find it difficult to display our private dreams in the way described above. This does not mean you cannot take advantage of the same energy. Instead of doing a treasure map that would be on show for all to see, you could build yourself a dream book, which could be kept private and taken out for you alone to look at. Decide on your vision and start to make a treasure map or dream book. You can do this with friends, colleagues or family for a communal vision, and it will enhance your relationships as well as help to manifest your vision.

EXERCISE: *A Treasure Collage of Your Goals*

Another version of the treasure map is to make a list of what you would like to achieve in a specified amount of time. For instance, if you are currently fifty years of age, you might have a list of sixty-five things you would like to achieve before you are sixty-five. You would then get yourself a clip frame and a pictorial or symbolic representation of each of your wishes. Paste the pictures and symbols as a collage onto a piece of paper and secure this in your clip frame. As you complete things on your list, you can stick on them a silver or gold star. Shaaron tends to use small silver stars for things that are fairly simple to achieve, for example: see Kevin Spacey live at the theatre; larger silver stars for things that are a little more challenging, for example: spend two months alone in the Outer Hebrides; and a gold star for the big challenges, for example: write a book and get it published.

The positive benefit of this is keeping in your mind the things you want to do, seeing your wishes being fulfilled and also awarding yourself stars.

GETTING READY FOR A LUCID DREAM

In order to attempt lucid dreaming you must be able to recall at least one dream each night. Once people realise the importance of dreams they readily start to remember them. Here are a few basic guidelines to help your powers of recall:

Ensure that you get plenty of rest, as the longer your sleep, the longer your dream period. We tend to experience our shortest dreams, which last about ten minutes, in the earlier part of the night. Dreams become progressively longer and they may last as long as an hour in the latter stages of sleep. Many people cannot recall their dreams when they wake and therefore say they do not dream. In fact everyone dreams, indicated by rapid eye movement, (REM), and the ones we remember are those we are having when we wake up. The later REM periods are likely to be four-

and-a-half, six, or seven-and-a-half hours after you go to sleep. One thing that will help is to set your alarm clock to go off during one of these periods.

* Water is the element of dreams and emotions. Drink a large glassful before you go to bed. This will wake you up as well as help you to remember.
* Do not have a heavy meal before you go to bed. Eat lightly, as early in the evening as possible, if you want to benefit from your dreams. In the ancient times they used to fast to trigger significant dreams.
* If you are physically exhausted you may be too deeply asleep to bring your dreams to consciousness.
* Do keep a notebook and pen handy so that you can immediately record your dream. This has the additional benefit of affirming to your unconscious mind that you intend to remember the messages it is sending you. Do not worry if you are unable to bring them back straight away. Stay still in the position you were in while you slept. Make your mind blank so that the dream can resurface. Failing this, focus on the feelings you woke with as this can help trigger the images.
* Keeping a dream journal helps you to understand the messages your dreams are sending you. When you read the dreams you have had over several nights or weeks you can see patterns emerging. Keeping a dream journal has another advantage: the more you record your dreams, the more likely you are to recall other ones that you have had during the night. If you seriously want to engage in lucid dreaming it is worth researching more information on keeping a dream journal.

Developing dream recall can sometimes be a slow process, but you will improve with consistent practice.

EXERCISE: *Lucid Dreaming*

For several days in succession, affirm your intention to have and remember a lucid dream on a specific date. At the same time, clearly and confidently state that you will remember to recognise that you are in a dream on that night.

Twice a day, as vividly as possible, imagine yourself recognising you are in a dream state. Also visualise your goal for the lucid dream. For example, you may decide to visit a beautiful tropical beach and witness a glorious sunset or sunrise. In the early days be very specific about what you want to experience and keep things simple.

Before entering a lucid dream, you need to have what is known as a 'dream-sign'. This is something that you can choose to see that confirms you are in a lucid dream. Make it something simple, say a full moon or some kind of symbol. Whatever you choose ensure that you include it when you are doing the visualisation stage.

1. Go to sleep at your normal time, but set your alarm for two hours earlier than usual. As soon as it goes off, get out of bed immediately and do something for half an hour. Then return to your bedroom and for the next half hour contemplate what you want to accomplish in your lucid dream. Remember to be very specific and keep it simple. Think about what you want to do, who you want to see or where you want to go.
2. Now return to bed and progressively relax yourself. First pay attention to your breathing and deepen it. Breathe in through your nose and take it all the way down into your stomach, then exhale through the mouth. Repeat this three times.
3. Then progressively tense and relax all the muscle groups starting with your feet. Bend them back and tense them, holding the position for ten seconds. When you let go, feel

the relaxation in that muscle group. Now tense them again, hold, and then relax. Repeat this with all the other muscle groups: legs, buttocks, back, abdomen, shoulders, neck, jaw, forehead, upper arms, forearms and wrists. After you have worked with each muscle group take a deep breath and let it out as a deep sigh. We release more tension in a sigh than in a normal breath.

4. Set your alarm again for two hours' time, or have someone wake you. If you do the latter, ensure that they know not to talk to you and to leave the room immediately so that they do not distract you.

5. Now simply relax and go to sleep. During this two-hour period you are likely to have at least one REM period of sleep, maybe even two.

When you believe you are in a lucid dream, look around you to find your dream-sign as confirmation. Then create your desired outcome.

CHAPTER 20

Opening the Third Eye

The third eye is the spiritual chakra in the centre of the forehead between the physical eyes. It has always been of extreme importance as it is the location of the inner eye: the part of us that looks into the realms of spirit. When this chakra is fully open and all its sections are operating clearly, it is like a crystal ball: an entry to other worlds and dimensions. Clairvoyance enables people to receive pictures from the spiritual worlds and to view the future. Seers were so called because they were the ancient Wise Ones who could see into people's hearts and into the future.

The third eye is also the storehouse of the wisdom we have acquired in past lives or experiences elsewhere. And when we send pure light out from this point, we can heal the minds and even the physical bodies of others.

Archangel Raphael is in charge of the development of the third eye for humanity. He is the patron saint of the blind, whether they are physically or spiritually unable to see, and helps everyone to open up their inner and outer vision. The Seven Veils of Illusion cover the third eye and the dance of the seven veils is a pictorial representation of the letting go of these illusions. When these have been dissolved you can find perfect spiritual clarity.

We are all born psychic to some extent and the way in which others respond to us affects whether we deny our gifts or develop them. Some people are fully clairvoyant at birth and maintain this ability. Others reopen suddenly in later life, but most seekers find that they gradually become more attuned. Intuition is a function of the third eye. While one person may see pictures, another will have flashes of knowing. Many people see colours when they start to open up or even a radiance round trees or people. It is possible to have your third eye fully operational without seeing vivid pictures, or fairies, angels and spirits. Everyone is different.

Looking After the Third Eye

Our body and chakras are a result of what we ingest. Certain things clog the third eye, especially if taken to excess, such as meat, fatty or processed foods, fruit and vegetables heavily contaminated with pesticides, sugar, cigarette smoke and alcohol. Obviously, pure, light, natural, fresh, organic food keeps the whole body alive and enables the delicate instrument of the third eye to operate at its optimum.

Constant worry, fear or over thinking clouds this chakra, while peaceful, harmonious living keeps it relaxed and working. Beautiful music relaxes and soothes the third eye, enabling it to function well, as does gentle exercise, meditation and quiet time. Amethyst crystal is deeply calming and delivers you to a state of receptive peace. Azurite assists you to face fears that bind you to your past. It then dissolves those fears, but this crystal should only be used when you are really ready to look into those areas of the psyche. Sugilite helps you to understand the lessons that your fears are teaching you in this lifetime. Used with gem silica, sugilite can also help you to understand and learn from fears from past and future lives.

To the Atlanteans, it was very important that the third eye remained pure and clear at all times. Amethyst and gem silica would be placed on the brow chakra to stimulate the third eye, to see beyond the illusions of time and space, and into the realm of spirit.

The Alta, the Magi and the Initiates would perform a daily exercise to help cleanse it and we can carry out these exercises today.

EXERCISE: *Release Fears from Your Past*

In Atlantis, they did not need to carry out this part of the exercise. Now, we are not as pure as the Atlanteans, so Kumeka has asked us to include this preliminary exercise so that you can benefit fully from the second and third parts.

Please do not do this exercise alone, as it can be unsettling. Have someone nearby that you can talk to afterwards if necessary.

Part I

PREPARATION EXERCISE: *Step 1*

When you feel ready to face your deepest fears, lie down – outside if possible – where you will not be disturbed, and ideally where you can hear the sound of water, but not the sea as this is too powerful. Near a stream, river or waterfall would be ideal, or even in your garden with the garden hose running so that the water is audible. If it is impossible to do this outside, imagine yourself in a beautiful place in nature by a running stream. The background sound of an indoor water fountain or the sound of flowing water on a CD would be helpful.

1. Lie down or sit back, and place an azurite crystal at your third eye. Close your eyes and concentrate on your breathing until you are relaxed.
2. Imagine the blue of the crystal moving slowly into your third eye until it reaches the centre.
3. Watch it stop for a moment, then slowly begin to rotate, and, as it does so, see its colour spread throughout the third eye. Allow the speed of the rotation to increase for as long as it feels comfortable. As soon as it begins to feel uncomfortable,

visualise its speed slowing slightly until it once again feels comfortable.

4. Allow the colour to rotate at this speed until it stops of its own accord. The time for which it rotates is unique to each person. Be aware that the rotating crystal is gathering information regarding your fears that bind you to your past.

5. Once the colour has stopped rotating, thank it, and let the blue return to the crystal.

6. Spend a few moments acclimatising to your body again and, when you feel ready, remove the crystal from your brow chakra.

7. Keep the crystal with you, and know that when you are ready it will release to your conscious mind information about your fears and help you to dissolve them. This information may come in dreams or into your thoughts during your daily business. Each time you are aware of one of these thoughts make a note of it. When you are able to do so, consider them and let them go.

PREPARATION EXERCISE: *Step 2a*

Each evening, before you go to bed, take time to lie down with a sugilite on your brow chakra. Ensure that you have a glass of pure water ready.

1. Concentrate on your breathing until you are relaxed.

2. In your mind's eye see the fear and ask the sugilite to help you to understand the lessons to be learned from it. Allow any thoughts or pictures to come into your mind.

3. If no thoughts or pictures appear, ask the sugilite to bring this information to you. See an envelope handed to you and accept it. Know that when you are ready, the information in the envelope will be revealed to you.

4. Allow yourself to get back in touch with your environment. Stretch a little. You can now drink some of your pure water.

Give yourself a few moments before you stand up. If you are still light-headed, then stamp your feet several times to help ground you. In future you might like to have a black tourmaline on the ground at your feet, to keep you grounded during this exercise.

PREPARATION: EXERCISE *Step 2b*

Once you understand the lessons of your fear and are ready to release them, you can lie down with the azurite on your brow chakra. Ensure that you have a glass of pure water ready.

1. Concentrate on your breathing until you are relaxed.
2. See the fear that you are ready to release, and visualise the colour of the azurite surrounding and enveloping the fear. Know the fear no longer has any hold on you.
3. See the colour return to the azurite.
4. Repeat this exercise until you have released all the fears that you are working with at this time.
5. When you have finished, allow yourself to return to full consciousness. Stretch a little. You can now drink some of your pure water. Give yourself a few moments before you stand up. As with the previous step, if you still feel ungrounded stamp your feet several times to help ground you, and in future try using a black tourmaline on the ground at your feet to keep you earthed during this exercise.

If you would like to do this exercise to deal with fears from past lives use azurite as above, then sugilite and gem silica together for revealing and understanding the lessons.

Part II

Assuming that you have successfully released your fears, you can now proceed to the second part of the exercise. This part of the exercise will allow you to awaken your inner senses and will particularly strengthen your ability to transmit accurately what you perceive when channelling, doing readings or counselling. The purer the quality of gem silica used, the greater the effectiveness that will be achieved. You will need two pieces of the crystal for this exercise.

1. Hold two pieces of gem silica, and lie down.
2. Place one on the brow chakra, and one on the throat chakra.
3. Close your eyes, and focus on your breathing until you feel relaxed.
4. Concentrating on the brow chakra, feel the energy from the gem silica enter your third eye. It is very powerful so as its energy enters your third eye you may feel your spine contract or you may need to take a deep breath. This is a sure sign that the energy is working with you.
5. Feel the pulsing energy exploring your third eye, expanding it, and relaxing it. Just allow the gem silica to do its work, it is cleansing and expanding your third eye.
6. When you are ready, become aware of the gem silica at your throat chakra and feel its pulsing power enter your throat.
7. Feel it explore, and radiate into your throat chakra and your vocal cords. Stay with this energy for a while.
8. After a few minutes, become aware of the two pieces of gem silica creating a circular motion around each other. The third eye sends its energy to the throat, which sends energy back to the third eye. Know that, in future, whatever you perceive with your third eye, you will be able to relay accurately to others. Whenever you wish to be a clear channel, just close your eyes and get in touch with this energy.
9. When you are ready, become aware of your surroundings and, slowly and gently, return yourself to the room.

10. Sit up slowly, drink your glass of water and give yourself a few moments to rest before standing up.

As before, if you feel light-headed, consider using a black tourmaline on the ground at your feet whenever you do this exercise.

Do this exercise at least once a week to keep the strength of the channel open.

Part III

Amethyst is the main stone for the third eye as it allows inner wisdom to be perceived. Doing this exercise on a regular basis will help to increase the strength of the signal that you receive. Additionally, amethyst will serve to keep your mind calm and untroubled. It will bring in peace and tranquillity. It is not unusual to fall asleep when doing this work with amethyst, but do not be concerned as the amethyst will continue its work regardless of whether or not you are aware of it.

1. Lie down and place your amethyst on your brow chakra. Close your eyes and concentrate on your breathing until you feel relaxed.
2. Concentrating on the brow chakra, feel the energy from the amethyst enter your third eye. You may also experience it enfolding your entire body and, possibly, a feeling of floating. This is usually a very nurturing feeling and you should enjoy it. Not everyone experiences this so do not worry if you do not.
3. Bring your attention back to the third eye and feel the energy of the amethyst. It is very soothing and relaxes your entire body. You can feel its healing energies moving through your mind, stilling it.
4. Know that the strength and quality of your connection with the clear purple ray of the amethyst is increasing.

5. Do this exercise as often as you like, for not only will it strengthen your link with the purple ray, but healing of your mind will also be taking place. The purple ray is majestic and highly spiritual energy that connects you to the Divine. A pleasant side effect of this work is that you will feel calmer and more at peace with the world.

6. When you are ready, become aware of your surroundings and, slowly and gently, return yourself to the room.

7. Sit up slowly, drink your glass of water and give yourself a few moments to rest before standing up.

Remember, if you feel light-headed or ungrounded, it may help to place a black tourmaline on the ground at your feet whenever you do this exercise.

CHAPTER 21

Astrology

Ordinary people did not need to understand the future or the cosmic influences on their lives exerted by the movement in the heavens. They lived in the eternal present knowing that the priesthood was looking after them. However, the Magi needed to understand these things, for they would be consulted to find, for example, a propitious day to start a building project. They used astrology and numerology in combination as a means of pinpointing the most auspicious dates for carrying out important functions.

Indeed, there is a correlation between astrology and numerology. In astrology for example, the First House is about developing the will and the personality. In numerology, the number 1 represents drive, individuality and determination. In both astrology and numerology, the number 1 indicates the beginning, the origin, the first, the birth.

The Magi also had to give fore-warning about eclipses, since the communities needed to know if the power of the moon and sun were to be diminished, so that all flying transports could be grounded.

Astrology, as we know it in the West today, has its origins in Mesopotamia and Egypt – the knowledge having been taken there by one of the twelve tribes that left Atlantis. Once there, it developed into different versions, but the basis and result would always be the same.

The karma with which we come into incarnation indicates the lessons we need to learn. These show up in our birth charts. Souls who come to Earth without karma should, in theory, have clear astrological charts, but they do not. The crystal and indigo children from Orion come in with no karma, but they have lessons marked in their charts. Kumeka says that these are not for the children, but for the growth and learning of the parents and family they are born to.

Atlanteans knew that as each being assumed a physical body, it began its chemical interaction with the cosmos. Additionally, they were aware that the time and place of birth imbued individuals with unique traits, skills and challenges. Atlantis was peopled over a period of a year to ensure they secured a balance of energies and elements, as well as the widest range of personality types and skills. By knowing his sun sign each individual would know which aspect of life he or she was working on. The sun indicates our purpose for this lifetime and it also denotes which lesson we are developing.

Sun Sign Definitions

Astrology is a vast and complex subject and we have, therefore, included only brief information about each sun sign and its purpose.

ARIES

The purpose of those born under this sign is to start projects and instigate new ideas. They are the captains, the leaders, the pioneers among people. Enterprise and ardour are characteristic qualities of this sign. These people tend to enjoy facing and overcoming difficulties, so they will generally do well in the battle of life – many of them finding themselves in a position to play a leading part. The driving force that moves them forward is hope for the future, though this can sometimes express itself as impatience and/or rebellion. The greatest success of an Arian is likely to be in the field of action and enterprise.

TAURUS

The purpose of those born under this sign is to produce and build. They tend to be stable and steadfast in character, understanding the importance of system and method. Known for their quiet persistence in the face of difficulties, they remain unshaken in adversity and refuse to be hustled or hurried, frightened or pushed into any false position, whether mental, physical, emotional or spiritual. They seek success in constructive work of a type that will endure, or is an achievement of permanent value to family or race. The driving force that motivates them is a desire for peace and stability. They seek to attain a secure resting place.

GEMINI

The purpose of those born under this sign is to make life more interesting and beautiful for themselves and others. They generally have intellectual energy, which must express itself, preferably in a variety of ways and often through experimental science, art and literature. They are constantly moving forward, looking for new mental challenges. They are likely to find success in the sphere of intellectual achievement or artistic expression – possibly in both. Many people under this sign have two callings, which may operate together or separate. Their driving force is an exuberance or overflow of energy, which seeks many outlets.

CANCER

The purpose of those born under this sign is to energise and inspire people by raising ideals. They can feel joy, sorrow, compassion, horror and every emotion, and they enable others to experience these too. They are home orientated and family is very important to them. Cancerians are teachers *par excellence*. These people are likely to find success in teaching or preaching, or in otherwise appealing to the imaginations and sympathies of their fellow man. Their style is picturesque, vivid and often very dramatic. Their driving force is the power that is associated with the growth, evolution and well-being of the race. Patriotism would be an example of this.

LEO

The purpose of those born under this sign is to instil courage and determination in others, and to encourage them to do their best. These people enjoy centre stage, though they have faith and trust in humanity and understand and appreciate the qualities of others. Their style is simple and straightforward, and their energy is ideal to head large enterprises, institutions or undertakings. Leos often find success in an area that gives them the chance to shine in the eyes of their fellow man. They want in some way to irradiate, brighten, inspire or harmonise the energies of others. The driving force of this sign is an abounding faith in the goodness of all things.

VIRGO

The purpose of those born under this sign is to teach purification through discrimination and attention to detail. They tend to be clear headed and thrifty, hard working and practical with clarity of vision and critical acumen. Many Virgos dedicate themselves to the service of others. Because of their desire to be perfect they are usually health conscious. These people need to find an outlet for the exercise of their keen powers of discrimination. They like an opportunity to give minute attention to apparently unimportant detail. It will probably be their duty to assist in some work of purification that is necessary for the healthy growth of the individual or state, or possibly some great public enterprise. The driving force of this sign is the desire for holiness, perfect purity or health: an impulse that causes them to strive for perfection.

LIBRA

The purpose of those born under this sign is to teach the skills of balance and partnership. Librans are naturally tactful, gracious, cheerful and polished. They are also impartial, compassionate, conciliatory and tender. They need to be involved in something that requires an all-round capacity rather than concentrated specialisation. If they do specialise it is likely to be in connection with music and the fine arts, or in some area that tends to beautify and to complete human life. The driving force for Librans is a desire for beauty and for balance.

SCORPIO

The purpose of those born under this sign is to teach others how to gain self-mastery. They are often quiet but have a resolute strength, will and determination. They are thorough, passionate and unflinching, commanding, analytical, authoritative and heroic. Many Scorpios are psychic but often fail to realise it. They are most likely to find success in an area that demands the exercise of concentration and personal magnetism. They will need work that is vitalising, regenerating or dominating in some way. The driving force of this sign is an excess of energy, which must find an outlet, preferably in the generation or creation of new forms, or in the destruction of the old and outworn.

SAGITTARIUS

The purpose of those born under this sign is to inspire people to seek for what is deepest in their soul and to come to an understanding of it. They enjoy travel, exploration, contact with other minds and enquiry into unfamiliar systems of philosophy, law or theology. Because of their extraordinary powers of mental activity, they need to be involved in work that requires the exercise of reason and development of the logical faculty. They enjoy getting to the bottom of things and take a genuine interest in the welfare and education of their fellow human. The driving force for this sign is the craving for wisdom and the determination to seek it out through the exercise of reason.

CAPRICORN
The purpose of those born under this sign is to teach a sense of history, tradition and authority. These are the diplomats or inter-mediaries, who desire a fixed standard of conduct and like to know their boundaries. They are traditional, conventional and goal orientated. They would find success in an area that gives them scope for personal or higher ambition, especially where there is a continuing possibility of promotion, and preferably where it can be seen by others. The driving force for this sign is reverence or devotion to the highest, giving an earnest desire to attain. It does not matter what they attain, the fact that they attain something is all that matters to them. They want the devotion or reverence from other people for having attained whatever it is.

AQUARIUS
The purpose of those born under this sign is to encourage others to expand their vision and push their boundaries. These are the truth seekers, often with an extraordinary breadth of vision. They tend to be unbiased, open-minded and without prejudice or superstition of any kind. They are patient, dispassionate and untiring. In their quest for truth, Aquarians should find success as an observer or recorder of phenomena and will probably engage in work that alters their outlook on life. The driving force for this sign is a craving for enlightenment and a passion for knowledge, especially of hidden truth that underlines the mystery of life.

PISCES
The purpose of those born under this sign is to show others how to be true to their inner convictions, regardless of outside influ-ences. The typical Piscean is sensitive and has little or no worldly

ambition, caring nothing for rank or power. They need to feel that their inner self has freedom to feel, dream, grow and evolve according to its own nature. This makes them indifferent to restrictions and limitations in this earthly life. These people will succeed in the field of self-sacrifice and renunciation. They will be aided by their intuitive knowledge of the spiritual world and the comparative unimportance of outward appearances and show. The driving force of this sign is love of the type that manifests as an intense craving for perfect union with the Beloved (the Higher Self, or Christ), which resides within each of us.

The Atlanteans recognised these as the general qualities and characteristics of the sun signs, but were, of course, aware that each person is also influenced by the position of the other planets at their birth and throughout that incarnation.

EXERCISE: *Why Was I Born?*
Using the information above as a guide, contemplate why your soul chose to be born under your particular sun sign. How do you express this energy in your life? How are you fulfilling your purpose?

EXERCISE: *Sun Sign Expression*
Find out the sun signs of members of your family and friends. How do they express their sun sign qualities? This could be done by yourself or together with the other person.

CHAPTER 22

Numerology

The people of Atlantis had some comprehension of the meaning of numbers, but the Magi, of course, fully comprehended the great cosmic influence that numbers have on our lives and destiny. As with astrology, this powerful tool was not needed for divination during the Golden Age, when everyone was automatically attuned to their spiritual path. However, the Magi used it with astrology to establish auspicious dates to, say, inaugurate a temple. Later, in the dark days, numerology was used to check and control the masses. Now, once again, the science of numbers is beginning to resume its rightful place as a tool for higher spiritual understanding.

Every number has a universal resonance and is an energy form. By the time it has descended to Earth, it has diluted considerably. Nevertheless, each number still emits a subtle emanation that affects your life path and your soul purpose. The number of every year affects you, as do the numbers of the letters of your names. People are drawn by magnetic attraction to houses of certain numbers or even car number plates. Certain dates are auspicious for particular events because of the cosmic influence of the numbers.

Like astrology, numerology is a vast and complex subject, so for the purposes of this book we will only give examples of the energies contained within each of the numbers.

Numerology deals with the single numbers 1 to 9, with the

exception of a few two-digit numbers that have special meaning. The letters of the alphabet correspond to numbers, each letter being assigned one according to its position in the alphabet. The table below indicates the letters of the alphabet and their numerical value.

Numbers assigned to the letters

1	2	3	4	5	6	7	8	9
A	B	C	D	E	F	G	H	I
J	K	L	M	N	O	P	Q	R
S	T	U	V	W	X	Y	Z	

Life Expression

The Atlanteans were aware that the vibration of your name has a profound significance in your life and resonates with the gifts and talents your soul has chosen to express. For this reason the incoming soul chooses its name, which it then telepathically imparts to its parents. While this was a conscious choice in the golden days, we now make these choices unconsciously. Every time your name is thought of, or spoken, the qualities of its number resonate in your life.

In Atlantis names were always spoken or sung lovingly, so that the child or adult felt safe and supported in the expression of his being. If you speak someone's name harshly or angrily, especially a child's, they will subtly perceive that it may be difficult to develop their potential.

TO FIND YOUR LIFE EXPRESSION
To understand what you are choosing to express in your life, take the full name you were given at birth, such as Janet Mary Smith, which we use in the example below. Take the number assigned

to each letter and add them up. This total is the numerological resonance of the name.

Example

J A N E T	M A R Y	S M I T H	
1+1+5+5+2	4+1+9+7	1+4+9+2+8	
14	21	24	
1 + 4 = **5**	2 + 1 = **3**	2 + 4 = **6**	= 5 + 3 + 6 = **14**

As numerology only uses single-digit numbers you will need to reduce a two-or three-digit number as follows. Let's use our example of Janet Mary Smith, which has the number 14. 1 + 4 = 5, so Janet Mary Smith becomes 5. Every time her name is thought or spoken the energies of number 5 will vibrate in her consciousness.

Here are some other examples:

37 would become: 3 + 7 = 10. 10 reduces further: 1 + 0 = 1
62 would become: 6 + 2 = 8
125 would become: 1 + 2 + 5 = 8

YOUR SIGNATURE
Remember, too, that the letters you use in your signature are extremely important, so do check out the numerology of your signature. Every time you sign it you are unconsciously calling in the energy of those letters.

The Energies of the Numbers 1 to 9

The energy of the number of your name has qualities and properties that reflect your personality and life path:

1 is independent, unconventional and individualistic. It represents the beginning, the source, the innovator, the originator, the instigator and the uniqueness. It is masculine, and represents a strong sense of courage and leadership. Ambitious and goal orientated, it has direction and does not doubt its course of action. High energy, dynamic force and a relentless drive towards its destiny are hallmarks of this number.

2 represents the peacemaker. It vibrates with co-operation, diplomacy and tact, and is the most gentle of all numbers, as well as the most resilient. Being the power behind the throne, it is supportive and often plays the role of advisor. It is very feminine and subtle, loving, vulnerable and humble, and has a love of music and harmony in any form. This number dislikes confrontation, is easily hurt and does not handle criticism well.

3 is the sunshine number. Central qualities are self-expression and communication. It enjoys life, does not take things too seriously and is the most playful of all the numbers. It has a happy-go-lucky number resonance, being both optimistic and enthusiastic. It is creative, inspirational and motivating, and with an energy that is expansive and outward moving – although often scattered – it lifts up those around it.

4 is the most practical of all the numbers, with a sharp eye for detail, and is orderly, systematic, methodical and precise. Reliable, punctual and dependable as well, it does what it says it will do. It is honest, trustworthy and totally without artifice. It also is rigid and dislikes change. It needs predictability and likes habits and rituals. It is the rock and the cornerstone, forming the foundation of every enterprise.

5 is the traveller's number. Adventurous and courageous, it is the most dynamic of all the numbers. It is persuasive, a promoter and an excellent sales person. Being versatile and adaptable, it is the experimenter and the explorer. It is also bright, quick witted and a straight shooter with extraordinary reflexes. It likes to juggle many projects but is easily distracted with a love for sensual pleasures and immediate gratification.

6 is most loving of all the numbers. As well as being committed, caring, sympathetic, protective and nurturing, it is also responsible, self-sacrificing and undemanding. It is domestic, maternal, family oriented and community conscious. It is the teacher and the healer, and cares for those who are weaker. It is visually artistic, creative and a craftsperson. It is the number of mother and fatherhood.

7 is the most spiritual of all the numbers and is the seeker of truth. It is also the number of the hermit. Cerebral, analytical, focused, contemplative and meditative; it is the intellectual and the abstract thinker; the accumulator of knowledge and wisdom. Often withdrawn and self-orientated, it is nevertheless insightful and understanding. It is an inward, interior journey with reflectivity, solitariness and quiet contentment.

8 is the number of the visionary and is the most result orientated of all the numbers. It represents balance between the material and the spiritual world. It is powerful, ambitious and money conscious and it understands money as a tool. It is the leader and the business person, with big dreams and huge plans. It is the overseer and the manager. With the strength and perseverance to see things through, it is understanding, forgiving and broad-minded. It is the gambler.

9 is the most humanitarian of all the numbers. It represents effort and sacrifice without the need for reward. It is giving, sharing, loving and caring. It is the statesperson, politician, lawyer, writer, philosopher and, above all else, the idealist. It has a worldwide consciousness and is the genius and the synthesizer. It is creative and artistic: the architect, landscaper, designer. It is noble, aloof, aristocratic and a healer of many.

Master Numbers

The numbers 11, 22, 33 and 44 possess more potential than other numbers. Being highly charged and difficult to handle, they require time, maturity and great effort to integrate them into a personality.

11 is the most intuitive of numbers, representing insight without rational thought, sensitivity, illumination and a channel to the subconscious. It is also the dreamer and is shy, impractical and nervous. The 11 walks that fine line between greatness and self-destruction. Its growth, stability and personal power is dependent upon its acceptance of intuitive understanding, or spiritual truths. Peace for the number 11 cannot be found in logic, but in faith – it is the psychic's number.

As 11 is also 2 (1 + 1 = 2) it has all the qualities of the number 2: charisma, leadership and inspiration. There is an inborn duality, which creates dynamism and inner conflict. Its mere presence tends to act as a catalyst.

22 is the most powerful of all numbers and is often referred to as the Master Builder. Potentially the most successful of all numbers, it is capable of turning ambitious dreams into reality. It has many of the inspirational and intuitive insights of 11, combined with the practicality and methodical nature of number 4 (2 + 2 = 4). It is unlimited and yet disciplined, bringing dreams into concrete form and making its visions manifest. If 22 does not use its gift of practicality, then it wastes its potential. Both 11 and 22 must set aside their personal ambitions and work towards the realisation of larger goals that are for the benefit of humankind.

33 is the number that resonates with Christ consciousness. It reduces to 6, which aims for togetherness and love.

44 is a sacred number, a Master Vibration, which resonates with the purity of Atlantis. It is the number of absolute balance of all the opposites and multi-levels. It offers a different way of seeing the universe, a complete and precise understanding of universal laws, and a way that could make possible a greatly-accelerated rate of human evolution. The colour of 44 is magenta.

44 reduces to 8, which is the number of infinity. 8 is the number that represents the balance between the material and spiritual world. It is also the number of the visionary. There are also 8 points to the brain, as described in the section on crystal skulls, in Chapter 25.

44 also represents the physical, emotional, mental and spiritual bodies and the 4 levels of consciousness: the conscious, subconscious, unconscious and superconscious. The conscious mind governs the physical world of awareness, while the subconscious contains the mental beliefs. The unconscious mind holds the emotional feelings and understandings. The superconscious is the spiritual level that knows all that is.

Life Path Number

There are challenges and lessons associated with each life path:

1. To learn about and experience independence, self-confidence and leadership.
2. To learn about and experience serving and supporting others, and being diplomatic.
3. To learn to experience, and bring to others, joy and wisdom through communication.
4. To learn to be stable, dependable, organised and practical, and demonstrate this to others.
5. To learn to have a flexible outlook and to use freedom constructively.

6. To learn to give and receive love wisely, and to create harmony in all situations.
7. To seek a deeper understanding of life and to spread this knowing wisely.
8. To learn how to harmonise the spiritual and material.
9. To learn to be selfless and compassionate, and to let go of that which no longer serves your growth.
11. To learn to accept intuitive understanding and to live by spiritual truths.
22. To work towards the realisation of impersonal goals and to serve the world in a practical way.
33. To learn the art of patience and right timing.
44. To accept and work with the purity that accelerates your ascension.

EXERCISE: *Find Your Life Path*

Using the date of your birth, the most important number in numerology, try this exercise to find your life path number.

Add the individual digits in the day, the month and the year of your birth. Total these numbers, and then reduce the resultant number into a single digit. Let's use the example of a person born on 26 January 1953:

Day	$2 + 6 =$	**8**
Month	$0 + 1 =$	**1**
Year	$1 + 9 + 5 + 3 = \mathbf{18}$ then $1 + 8 =$	**9**
		$\mathbf{18} = 1 + 8 = \mathbf{9}$

The life path number is 9.

The date of birth is reduced to a single digit in this way except when it is one of the master numbers: 11, 22, 33 and 44. It has been known for people to manipulate the mathematics in order to arrive at a master number, but bear in mind that these numbers represent an extremely challenging lifetime.

Soul Urge Number

This shows you the dreams closest to your heart and therefore the underlying motive in what you do. Add together the numerical value of the vowels only in your name. Reduce them to single digits and then add the single digits together. Remember to keep the master numbers as double digits, as shown in the following example. Also note that a Y is also a vowel when there is no other vowel in a syllable – Lynn or Carolyn, for example, and when it is preceded by a vowel and sounded as one sound, like Hayden. A W is treated as a vowel when it is preceded by a vowel and produces a single sound, as in such names as Bradshaw.

EXERCISE: *Find Your Soul Urge Number*

Example 1: Using 'Y' as a Vowel

PETER		HENRY		JONES	
$5 + 5$		$5 + 7$		$6 + 5$	
$= 1 + 0 = 1$	$+$	$= 1 + 2 = 3$	$+$	11	$= 15 = 1 + 5 = 6$

The Soul Urge number in this instance is 6.

Example 2: Using the 'W' as a Vowel

ANN		SHAW	
1		$1+5$	
1	$+$	6	$= 7$

The Soul Urge number in this instance is 7

Your Balance Number

This number tells you how you tend to respond to life and its changes.

EXERCISE: *Find Your Balance Number*
Add together the value of the initials of all your names and reduce this number to a single digit. For this exercise the master numbers will also be reduced to a single digit because they reflect a talent or a special ability, whereas your balance number indicates an attitude or an approach.

Example
Peter Henry Jones would be:

P		H		J			
7	+	8	+	1	=	**16**	1 + 6 = **7**

The Balance number in this instance is 7.

Enhancing Numbers with Crystals.

Each number has its own frequency, which can be enhanced by working with the corresponding vibrations from the mineral kingdom. Using appropriate crystals can help you to understand and complete your lessons for this lifetime. Here are some examples:

1. Aquamarine, larimar, turquoise

2. Sapphire, smoky quartz, watermelon tourmaline

3. Amethyst, chrysoprase, lapis lazuli

4. Ametrine, kyanite, clear quartz

5. Blue lace agate, carnelian, prehnite

6. Citrine, labradorite, topaz

7. Fluorite, kunzite, rose quartz

8. Celestite, opal, selenite

9. Chalcedony, pietersite, imperial topaz

11. Jade

22. Galena

33. Black coral

44. Iris agate

CHAPTER 23

Healing

Perfect health was the norm in Golden Atlantis. In the very early times, healer priests merely needed to keep people's mental, emotional and spiritual bodies in alignment so that the physical body could demonstrate perfect vitality and balance.

Spiritual healing was practised in Atlantis in much the same way as it is today. The principles were the same, but the people were such pure channels for the energy that the effect was more immediate and lasting. Just as now, everyone was capable of healing at some level, and the more evolved and trained they were, the clearer the channel and the stronger the healing. Intention and love were, and still are, the most important factors.

When your heart centre opens, you start to feel tingling in your hands, and this is the first indication many people have nowadays that they are healers. In early Atlantis everyone's heart was open. Spiritual energy flowed through them constantly and so, of course, they were all able to give each other divine healing.

One of the agreements your soul makes on visiting Earth is that if you owe a debt when you leave, you must come back to repay it. This is the Law of Karma. In the halcyon days, at the beginning of the Golden Age, everything was kept in balance, so there was nothing owing when you died. Your soul was free to move on. Within generations it became more difficult to stay in total balance and people occasionally left with a karmic debt in their soul records. When that person reincarnated, this would show up as an emotional or mental blockage and would inevitably develop into a physical problem in the course of time. Naturally this was more difficult to rebalance and more advanced healing methods were required.

Use of Herbs

The Atlanteans were highly-knowledgeable herbalists and understood the properties of medicinal plants. All of nature is built according to sacred geometry, so each herb contains a specific geometric structure, and so does every part of the human body. If an area of the mental, emotional or physical body is out of synch with its divine blueprint, illness will result. Atlanteans knew which herb had the same geometric structure as, and vibrated perfectly with, each part of the body. If eaten, that herb would seek out the blueprint of the damaged organ within the body and align, heal and regenerate it.

The healer priests became extremely skilled in the preparation and application of useful plants. Plants were always picked at optimum times of the day or night, in accordance with the moon cycle, so that their life force was at its peak. One of the ways the women of Atlantis used their innate wisdom was as herbalists, for which they were highly respected. It was not until the fall that they were branded as witches.

Crystals

Crystals operate in a similar way: the vibration of a stone will always endeavour to harmonise the natural world to its higher energy including people. Of course, different crystals have varying qualities and properties. The Atlanteans were aware of this and were able to use the appropriate ones to heal or attune people. They were able to add energy by powering the stones with refracted light, reflected from facets of other crystals. The number of facets governed the amount of power that came through.

If, for example, someone cut their arm, the molecules in the nerves and tissue were disrupted. The Atlanteans matched the power in a laser crystal to the correct vibration of the area of the wound. When the crystal was focused on it, the pain ceased immediately and the wound would heal without a scar as the molecules moved into the correct geometric structure.

Crystal chambers were used to speed up or slow down cellular rate to that required for healing. These days we hold in the human collective unconscious a belief that it is impossible to regrow limbs. Because the Atlanteans had no such restriction in their beliefs, they were able to regenerate limbs by placing people in crystal chambers vibrating at the frequency of the tissue. These could re-establish the correct cellular rate, enabling growth to take place. They assisted this process by holding in their minds a picture of the perfectly grown limb. Also, a person ages because his vibration slows. The frequency of the crystal chambers would speed up the cellular vibratory rate and allow rejuvenation to take place, especially when used in conjunction with the Mahatma Energy (see Chapter 14).

Crystals were also positioned to receive healing resonance from other planets. The beings on the Pleiades still send constant healing to us. During Atlantean times, the healing energy was downloaded into smaller crystals to help balance people and keep them healthy.

Colour and sound both vibrate at various frequencies. Higher frequencies produce colour, and as they are lowered they become sound. These vibrations were passed through crystals to focus the energy and enable cellular healing to take place. Focused sound, for instance, was vibrated through a broken bone to facilitate its joining and healing.

If someone felt homesick for his planet of origin – a condition that we might call mild depression – he would go to a sound chamber, or to a specific concert, and listen to glorious, inspirational music, which would lift his spirits again.

Musically-gifted people would tone into the chakras to cleanse them and bring them into balance again. Other people lay in pools of water coloured with vegetable dye to absorb the energy of the colour. This form of healing is still available to us today – simply find the appropriate colour of vegetable dye, add it to a warm bath and relax for half an hour. Playing relaxing music and burning appropriate oils also enhances the experience. Following are the colours and their properties.

- **Red** to energise you.
- **Orange** for friendliness and sociability, and to balance your sexuality. It also encourages creativity.
- **Yellow** for calming and expanding the mind and allowing you to think more clearly. It also makes you feel stronger.
- **Green** to help to balance and centre you.
- **Pink** to harmonise your heart, especially if you feel hurt, and to bring you feelings of unconditional love. It also develops a deep sense of right and wrong.
- **Turquoise** to enable you to have clearer communication and to speak with integrity.
- **Deep Blue** to quieten and still your mind, inspire you, develop your intuition and allow you to open up to spiritual visions.
- **Violet** to bathe you in the pure spiritual light of enlightenment.

Aromatherapy

In Atlantean times, aromatherapy was commonly used for healing the spirit, while also restoring emotional and mental balance, and was carried out in many ways. In fact they employed massage, inhalation, ointments, compresses and fragrant baths just as we do now.

Illnesses are invariably a result of mental or emotional imbalances that have ultimately manifested physically, so we share with you a few blends that treat some of these imbalances. Since essential oils today, as in Atlantean times, are very pure, great care should be taken with them. Because of this, only use the suggested blends below in a burner unless you are a qualified practitioner. Do not use them in any other way. The appropriate number of drops should be added to the water in the well of the burner. This should then be left in a room with you over the next hour or so. At intervals take in a deep, slow breath.

- If you are analytical and detached you can add warmth to your spirit with 3 drops of geranium, 2 drops of sandalwood and 1 drop of patchouli.
- Agitated, nervous people would be calmed by a blend of 3 drops of lavender, 2 drops of neroli and 1 drop of bergamot.
- Determination can be increased by using 4 drops of cedarwood and 2 drops of ginger.
- Energise your mind and rid yourself of tedium with 3 drops of coriander, 2 drops of patchouli and 1 drop of bergamot.
- Enliven your spirit with 3 drops of jasmine, 1 drop of ylang-ylang and 1 drop of orange.
- If you are forgetful, let 3 drops of pine, 1 drop of lemon and 1 drop of rosemary help to restore a clearer memory.
- Frustrated, irritable people would benefit from 2 drops of orange, 2 drops of bergamot and 2 drops of chamomile.
- If you are negative, tense and frustrated, calm yourself with 3 drops of bergamot, 2 drops of orange and 1 drop of neroli.
- Overburdened and humourless people would benefit from 3 drops of lemon and 2 drops of jasmine.
- Patience and tolerance can be restored by the use of 3 drops of bergamot, 2 drops of lavender and 1 drop of peppermint.
- Positive feelings could replace negativity and pessimism with the regular use of 2 drops of hyssop, 2 drops of clary sage and 2 drops of orange.

- Lack of self-worth can be eased by the regular use of 2 drops of rose and 2 drops of jasmine.
- Morale can be boosted with the use of 2 drops of thyme, 2 drops of pine and 2 drops of cedarwood.
- If you are obsessively worried or your mind is constantly over-thinking, then 4 drops of sandalwood and 2 drops of vetiver would help to calm your overactive mind.
- Resistance to change can be reduced by using 3 drops of cypress, 2 drops of juniper and 1 drop of benzoin.
- Restless and distracted people would find peace and focus by using 3 drops of frankincense and 2 drops of geranium.
- Sudden bouts of fearfulness would be assisted by using 2 drops of geranium, 2 drops of vetiver and 1 drop of rose.
- Tense and exhausted people would respond to 3 drops of clary sage, 2 drops of cypress and 1 drop of lavender.

EXERCISE: *Relaxing with Essential Oils*
1. Choose an appropriate blend from the list above.
2. Sit in the room near your burner, close your eyes and take a deep breath.
3. Smell the aroma as it passes through your nasal receptors and know that it is working with your mind and spirit to affect your being positively.
4. Remain relaxed in your chair and, whenever it feels right to you, take another deep breath.

It is really effective to do this for short periods of time – say half an hour – on a frequent basis, daily if possible.

EXERCISE *Healing*
If you wish to practise healing, here are some simple steps. It is vital that the healing comes from spirit and not through your own energy – which it may if your ego is involved. If you really want the other person to be healed then your ego is coming into play.

Remember that the angels may direct the healing into the other person's mental, spiritual or emotional body, not his physical one. You must be detached from the result and accept the divine will. You are merely the channel. Make sure you have your partner's full permission to give healing. If you are going to touch his crown chakra you should check that this is all right before you do so.

1. Ask the person you are working with to sit sideways on a chair, so you can reach his back and front.
2. Place your hands on his shoulders and say a little prayer, offering yourself in divine service. The shoulders are connected to the feet chakras, which open and help to keep the person you are healing grounded.
3. Visualise both of you in a bubble of protection.
4. When you feel the healing energy flowing, move your hands to where you feel it is needed. You can work on the physical body or in the aura an inch or two (3–5 cm) away. If in doubt start at the top and move your hands over each of the chakras in turn, down the back and then down the front of the body.
5. Hold the person's feet for a few moments. This is comforting and helps to bring the Divine Energy down through his body.
6. It is lovely to stroke down his aura very gently when you have finished.
7. Stand behind him again with your hands on his shoulders and thank the spiritual realms for any healing that they have channelled through you.
8. Detach yourself from the other person and from the results of the healing by shaking and flicking any of the person's energy from your hands.

EXERCISE: *Toning into Chakras One to One*
You will need to do this with one person. (We suggest that you
don't eat garlic just before you do this!)

Toning is the making of any sound. You can make an *aaahh*
sound or an *ohm,* or whatever sound comes easily and naturally
to you. The most important thing is that you open yourself up to
the angels and ask them to work with the sound that comes
through you. The only thing that can hold you back is ego, in
other words the belief that your personality is doing this. When
you hold the intention of being a pure channel for spirit, then the
perfect sound for healing or aligning the other person will come
from you. This means that when you tone, you ask the angels of
healing to use the sound you are making for the highest good of
the person you are working on. Your task is to set your intention
and allow a harmonious note to come through you. You do not
have to be able to sing or be particularly musical.

1. Talk to the person that you are going to work with. Ascertain
   whether he would like a general balancing or if one chakra
   needs more energy than the others. If he says he has a sore
   throat, for example, you will know that his throat chakra is
   depleted; if he indicates indigestion, his sacral chakra or his
   solar plexus may need more attention.
2. Ask your partner to stand, sit or lie down. If sitting, he
   should be sideways on a chair so that you can reach the
   chakras at the front and back. If he is lying, start down the
   front and he will have to turn over for you to tone into the
   chakras at the back.
3. Centre yourself by taking a few deep breaths, and relax your
   throat.
4. Remember, before you make any sound dedicate your
   intention to rebalance or heal this person for the highest
   good and ask the angels of healing to work through your
   voice.

5. Take in a breath and tone, as explained above, into your partner's crown chakra. Your mouth should be from three to eight inches (8–20 cm) from the body.
6. When you have finished, move down to the third eye and then the throat. You can do either the front first or the back.
7. If you started with the front chakras, now work down the back ones.
8. Take time to share what each of you experienced.

EXERCISE: *Toning into Chakras in a Group*
The same principles apply. Choose one person whose chakras you wish to balance, heal or energise and ask him to sit against a wall, or sit or lie in the middle of the circle.

1. Let the person tell the group where he would like you all to focus extra attention.
2. Give him a moment or two to be relaxed and receptive.
3. Everyone in the healing group should centre by taking a few deep breaths and relaxing their throats.
4. Remember, before you make a sound dedicate the intention to rebalance or heal this person for the highest good and ask the angels of healing to work through your voices.
5. All take in a breath and tone towards the person you are working with, as explained above. Mentally direct the sound to his crown chakra.
6. When you have finished, direct the sound to the third eye and then the throat. You can do either the front first or the back.
7. If you started with the front chakras, now work down the back ones.
8. Take time to share what each of you experienced.

CHAPTER 24

Working with Crystals

Throughout all the experiments in Atlantis, crystals played a major part in the everyday lives of the people, as well as having specific and special roles to play in areas like healing and ceremony, and as providers of energy. The following chapters will show you how they were used and give you exercises so that you can use this knowledge and begin to harness their purity and power to improve your life.

A crystal comes to you when you are ready for it. This can happen in a number of ways. It may come to you as a gift, you may find one, it may appear in your home or, more commonly, you may be attracted to one that you buy.

Crystals and Computers

People in western society are predominantly left brained, since reading, technology, intellect and rational thinking are prized today beyond creative and artistic expression or original concepts. However, with the advent of the New Age, this is beginning to change. Ideally, the capacity of both sides of the brain should be equally balanced and when this happens, we will once again produce super beings with highly developed mental capacity.

In the recent past, humans wrote lists, facts and figures on paper. They made calculations and deductions in their heads or by writing them down. All this laborious work used the left hemisphere of the brain – the masculine side of the mind. It is interesting that computers, using silicon chips from quartz crystal to store memory, have now been developed to do all this repetitive work that is based on logic and deduction.

The spiritual realms had a higher spiritual purpose for allowing computers to be developed on Earth now. They believed it would leave more time for humans to use the right hemisphere of the brain – the feminine, creative, psychic and spiritual side.

So far we have not responded to this opportunity. Instead we have allowed computers to speed time up. For example, before the advent of computers an individual might have written eight letters in a morning, now he can dispatch eighty separate e-mails and copy them to thousands more recipients. This, of course, not only sends out many times more communications in the time frame, but also generates infinitely more left-brain work. Modern computer-literate humans have speeded time up tenfold. This was not the spiritual intention. In Atlantis the crystal computers did the left-brain work, while people used their remaining time to relax, contemplate, connect with nature, enjoy life and create.

Crystal Power

Atlanteans used crystals for almost everything. They were the source of their power and awesome technology. Crystals have a consciousness. They are in touch with each other. They have the ability to retain, maintain and transfer the intensity of energy in order to focus and transit it over great distances.

The highly-evolved Atlanteans used crystals to enhance healing, awaken and develop psychic abilities, and to enable people in meditation to connect with Source. The divine energy locked within crystals helped them to increase their mental capacity and focus their thoughts with clarity. Great quartz generator crystals aided the Atlanteans in the dematerialisation of objects and in teleportation. Quartz crystals also helped with telekinesis, the levitation and transport of objects, especially large blocks of stone. Huge crystal towers or pyramids powered the communication networks and energy grids of Atlantis, and also controlled the weather.

Crystal Layouts

Atlanteans used particular crystal layouts for birthing: clear quartz to empower and enliven, rose quartz to develop a loving heart, blue lace agate to calm and sooth, and turquoise to aid open and honest communication. They also created caves of crystal. If, as a result of a medical check up, a person was discovered to have a particular imbalance, the healer would take him to spend time meditating in one of these crystal caves. The crystal would be specific to his needs.

Crystal layouts were put round people at night for healing or relaxation. These spreads would also encourage their spirit to fly to a preferred destination during their sleep. Or they might programme the crystals to enable them to visit a particular being of light for instruction, purification or some other purpose. Many of the Illumined Ones and archangels will help you in your dream state, if you instruct your spirit to visit them.

Birth Crystals

While souls were being born into Atlantis, the crystals they needed to link them back to their homeland would materialise. Because of the Veil of Amnesia, people could hold their crystals and feel good, but they would not have any memory of their homeland. However, during their incarnation, if their spirits wanted to visit their base planet they could do so while they were asleep. In that case, these special birth crystals, laid out round their body, would help to propel their spirit on its way. The crystals came with them from their planet of origin and, after their death, would dematerialise and return home with them. We do not have these crystals on Earth now.

In current times it is often not permitted for people to visit their planet of origin, even in sleep. It is considered that the longing to return would prevent them from fully participating in their mission on Earth. So now, people are often attracted to wear moldavite, an extraterrestrial meteorite, which links them to the cosmos, while helping them to feel grounded and rooted here.

Record Keeper Crystals

The Atlantean historians retained the records of what was happening on Earth in their minds. They were specially trained and the capacity of their memory banks was extraordinary. This was a role generally undertaken by women. In due course they programmed all this information into record-keeper crystals, using thought power.

We use the crystals within computers today to store records and other knowledge, much the same way that they did thousands of years ago. Those ancient record-keeper crystals – which still contain all the sacred Atlantean knowledge – occasionally turn up, and people of sufficiently high consciousness can telepathically draw the information from them, by placing them on their third eye and allowing the programmes to be downloaded.

Over the past few thousand years history has been written by the victors of power struggles and is highly subjective, even distorted. In Atlantis, the information programmed into keeper crystals was objective and honest.

Appropriate crystals were programmed to help with the growth of plants. They were also able to work with the magnetic force fields of plants, trees, seeds or any living thing, in order to strengthen its energy.

Crystal Co-operation

A crystal is a living, elemental energy. The heart-centred Atlanteans had a sense of oneness with all things, so they were able to connect their frequency with that of the crystal's elemental energy and ask it to light up. Because of the love connection, as well as the mental attunement, the crystals responded. The heart was the power and the mind was the switch.

The houses were illuminated in this way, by pure, clean and free crystal light. They were also used in the healing temples where the priest switched them on. However, crystal light was not just a form of illumination; when the crystals lit up their power was increased.

We are told that it is now possible for some people to do this again. Indeed, Diana has spoken to people who have, on occasion, enabled a crystal to light up. One lady told her that she could switch on her large quartz crystal and it would light up the room. Another, that she could command her amethyst to come to light. Diana was also told this story, by someone we will call Jean, who lives in Devon, England. Jean said that her son had been going through a difficult time, so she gave him a beautiful rose quartz crystal. Of course, rose quartz resonates with the heart chakra. He kept it by his bedside and a few days later his girl-friend was woken by glorious pink light emanating from the crystal and filling the room. She woke him immediately and they both saw it. We assume that the love of the mother, and the love the couple had for each other, was enough to switch the crystal on and power it.

In early Atlantis, when the consciousness was high and pure, crystal power provided heat, refrigeration and power to homes and towns. Furthermore, crystal technology enabled the people of Atlantis to travel at speeds unimaginable to us in our current state of scientific discovery. How could this be? It is quite simple. The crystals were asked to co-operate, they agreed, and were then programmed to carry out the necessary work. There is great power in spiritual purity.

The Initiates would leave their bodies in special rooms made of crystals when their spirits were travelling. Crystal power acted as a boost and protected their physical bodies while they were away. Often, if they knew it was their time to die, the Initiate would simply leave his or her physical body there, never to return.

Atlantean Seed Crystal

Atlantean seed crystals are flawless crystals that symbolise the spiritual law: As Above, So Below. They were found growing in the ground in the same way that flowers do. The Atlanteans never received without giving something in return, so they were often given as gifts, and, as the seed crystals were used for healing the heart, they were popular presents.

EXERCISE: *Encouraging Right-brain Activity*

This is an exercise to encourage right-brain activity. You will need one of each of the following crystals: black tourmaline for grounding, chrysocolla for creativity, smithsonite (lavender-violet) for psychic ability, amethyst for balance and imperial topaz (also known as golden topaz) for spirituality.

If possible, sit on the floor cross-legged. If this is not comfortable, sit on a chair with your feet flat on the floor.

1. Place the black tourmaline at the soles of your feet.
2. The other four crystals are going to form a square round you:
   * The amethyst at the front-left corner, by your left knee.
   * The imperial topaz behind you to the right.
   * The smithsonite behind you to the left.
   * The chrysocolla at the front-right corner, by your right knee.
3. Ensure that you are within the square at all points (see diagram below).
4. Place your hands in your lap with the palms open and facing upwards.
5. Close your eyes, take three long, deep, slow breaths and then, in your mind's eye, visualise the energy of each of the crystals at the four corners stretching out to the crystal to its right:
   * The amethyst's energy goes to meet the chrysocolla.
   * The chrysocolla's energy goes to meet the topaz.
   * The topaz's energy goes to meet the smithsonite.

Layout of crystals to expand the right brain

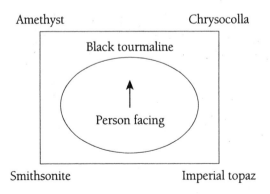

- The smithsonite's energy goes to meet the amethyst. You are now surrounded by the energy of the crystals. Picture the energy from each crystal rising upwards and inwards so that it meets above your head forming a pyramid in which you are enclosed.
6. Now feel the crystal light fill the space in which you are sitting. Feel it all around and through you, imbuing you with its energy.
7. Sit like this for at least two minutes, or longer if you prefer.
8. Do this exercise regularly and notice your right-brain activities of creativity, channelling, divine connection, artistic expression and openness, beginning to manifest in your life.

CHAPTER 25

Crystals in Atlantis

Crystal Skulls

The crystal skulls have fascinated people for centuries. It has always been understood, in esoteric circles, that they were fashioned in Atlantis and hold great secrets, which will only be returned to humanity when we are ready.

In the golden times, twelve crystal skulls were created by mind control and thought power. Each one came from a solid piece of quartz, and there was one for each tribe of the twelve regions. This particular shape was chosen to hold the sacred information after much deliberation. It was considered by the High Priests and Priestesses, in consultation with the Intergalactic Council, that the human skull was an expression of consciousness, the container of the most sacred part of man. Humans revered it as the house of the soul, the intellect and the personality. The choice of this part of the physical body also symbolised the ability of the spirit to journey and the power of the soul to travel to other worlds.

Each of these skulls was the size of our human skull and had a jaw that moved, so they were able to speak and sing. Within the crystal was a network of prisms and lenses, which lit up the beauty of the face and eyes.

The crystal skull was an advanced computer, and each of the twelve skulls contained all the knowledge that their tribe had gathered. The High Priests and Priestesses also programmed into the crystal skulls the knowledge of human origins and the mysteries of life. This, and much more, was stored within the oddly shaped computers so that future generations of humanity could understand these concepts when they were ready. This will be when humans who are sufficiently sensitive can tune into the skulls' very high rate of vibration and 'read' the contained information.

Often at great personal risk, the priestesses of the temples took their sacred skulls with them when they left Atlantis, just prior to its final destruction. The twelve are hidden somewhere on the planet.

So far, one has been found: the Mayan skull. In 1927, a young girl, Anna, was helping her father, the archaeologist, Dr F. A. Mitchell-Hedges, to explore one of the lost Mayan cities, deep within the rainforests of the ancient ruin of Lubaantum. This was in the British Honduras, now Belize, a country situated on the Caribbean between Mexico and Guatemala. She discovered the skull under an altar and has been its keeper ever since.

Because the skull was fashioned with powers long lost to us, scientists can find no scratches to indicate that it was carved with metal instruments. Even with diamond-tipped tools and our most advanced technology it has been estimated that it would take 300 years of constant work to grind the skull from a solid block of quartz. Of course, scientists are looking for the explanation through physical technology rather than spiritual technology.

This skull has been accredited with strange powers. Sensitives sometimes see an aura round it, or smell a sweet-sour odour. People hear sounds like tinkling bells or a choir of voices, emanating from it. Many have had visions and claim its powers help with healing and prophecy.

Other crystal skulls that have been discovered are not Atlantean. They were fashioned in Egypt by the Magi of the tribes that left Atlantis and went to Egypt. The information they contain is not as perfect and pure as that contained in the original twelve skulls.

There was also a thirteenth skull, fashioned in exactly the same way, but this time from amethyst. This skull contained all the knowledge and wisdom that the twelve skulls held. It is of a very high frequency, so it has dematerialised and is invisible to humans at our current level of evolution. It is in the charge of the Sphinx, which is its keeper on Earth. When all twelve skulls have been retrieved, and are brought together with eight specific quartz wands, the thirteenth, the amethyst master skull, will be released by the Sphinx. Until this time it will remain hidden.

In the layout below, the circular shape symbolises All That Is. Each skull contains the spiritual knowledge of the Atlantean tribe it represents and the eight quartz wands correspond to the eight parts of the cranium (or brain box) of the human skull: occipital, parietal left, parietal right, frontal, temporal left, temporal right, sphenoid and ethmoid, thereby indicating wisdom. When the amethyst skull is added to the crystal layout, the pure energy of Golden Atlantis will return to the Earth. The basis of this layout

The cyrstal skull layout

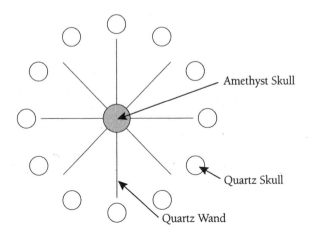

Amethyst Skull

Quartz Skull

Quartz Wand

is shown, but at this time we are not allowed to know the direction the skulls and wands will face. We are still not considered sufficiently evolved to use this power wisely.

Atlantean Energy Crystals

Over recent years, crystals that are specifically here to usher in the Atlantean energy have been found around the world. Until now they have been known as the New Age crystals. These stones, which are arriving to serve us, are willing to contribute their life force to help us take one of the most important steps in the course of our history. When we learn to attune ourselves to them, they will exercise a subtle and powerful effect on our psyche and energy system. Then we will be able to move into a more advanced system of healthcare, as well as a higher way of being. However, the conscious energy within the crystals requires a commitment from us: to express and share more love on a daily basis so that the earth can reverse its destructive course.

Crystals have been used as a tool for healing for centuries, but those appearing now are specifically for our current times. They are here to help with the many physical, emotional and mental problems that result from the energies and influences of today. Additionally, they have come to show us what may appear to be new possibilities of consciousness and lifestyle, but which are, in fact, the Atlantean energies returning to the planet. Colours and energies that we have been unable to perceive before are now being reflected in these crystals. More of these crystals are being discovered all the time. Below, we have listed some of them together with the lessons they offer and how they can serve you. (Note: Crystals without an asterisk are working with Atlantis as one of many of their tasks. These are the crystals that are indigenous to earth. Crystals with one asterisk are not indigenous to Earth but have been sent here to help us raise the vibration ready for the return of the pure energy of Atlantis. Crystals with two asterisks, foundation crystals, are of a high frequency and have been on Earth serving us for some time. They are working very consciously and actively towards bringing back Atlantis, which is a high priority for them.)

AMETHYST**

The Amethyst teaches humility. Ego, which is basically any belief or thought that keeps you separate from others, is holding many people back. When you learn to be humble, without ego, the powers of the universe can direct and guide you. The amethyst reminds you to let go and trust. This gentle crystal shows you that when you give everything up, you are open to receive more. Then the Divine can fill you with wisdom and love.

ANGELITE

This crystal helps you to develop compassion and to accept that which cannot be changed. When resistance dissolves, your stuck energy is freed. Then angelite can raise your awareness and heighten your perception. It will deepen your levels of attunement and connect you to universal knowledge.

AZEZTULITE

This sacred crystal only comes to you when you are ready. It then expands your consciousness and raises your vibration. It attunes you to the highest frequencies to which you are able to connect and accelerates your spiritual evolution.

BLACK OBSIDIAN

Black indicates the secret, mysterious and unknown. It also holds the potential of what we can be. This is a very powerful crystal, so please do not underestimate its power. It brings up whatever it is you need to look at, so you need to be ready! It does not take account of human fragility. For example, black obsidian helps you to bring hidden aspects of your ego, such as your selfishness, fear or rigidity, to the light of awareness. As you release the darker aspects of your unconscious self, you can function more happily in the material world. Your magnificence, if you hide it, will also be drawn forward.

CELESTITE

This celestial crystal can stimulate spiritual development by opening a connection to the universal energies. It helps to balance intellect with instinct, enabling people to align themselves in total harmony. This is the stone of enlightenment, as its subtle influence allows you to trust in the Infinite. You can place celestite in any room of your home where you wish to raise the vibration.

CITRINE QUARTZ**

The wonderful golden citrine is the stone of abundance. It energises you and fills you with life force so that you can attract your heart's desire into your life. Using a citrine sphere will help deepen your meditative state.

FLUORITE*

This beautiful extraterrestrial stone is mind expanding. It teaches you to release the illusion of the third-dimensionally-created world and to let your mind reach into the spiritual realms and become interdimensional. It is often called the 'genius stone' because it helps to balance negative and positive aspects of the consciousness, to enable you to grasp cosmic concepts and the spiritual laws of the universe.

GEM SILICA (GEM-QUALITY CHRYSOCOLLA)

This is the peace crystal, which subtly helps you to release suppressed feelings and become more vulnerable, open and sensitive. When you develop these qualities you can never harm yourself or another. Furthermore, it inspires people to develop qualities of patience, kindness, tolerance, compassion and humility, which will ultimately pave the way for planetary peace.

KUNZITE

Kunzite connects you with your soul. It promotes emotional balance by helping you to let go of the fears and sorrows that bind you to the past. And it connects you with your inner heart, which is an infinite source of love: your own divine essence.

LARIMAR

This soft blue stone is here to help with the healing and evolution of the earth. It brings serenity, peace, tranquillity and spiritual empowerment, so that you can safely develop your creativity and joy. It helps the soul onto its true pathway by gently healing any trauma in your past and encouraging your playful, childlike essence to emerge. Part of its service is to help harmonise your body and soul to new vibrations.

MOLDAVITE*

This powerful extraterrestrial crystal connects you to your higher purpose at all times and therefore accelerates spiritual growth and facilitates the ascension process. When you work with moldavite it helps you to access the Akashic Records. This stone currently helps indigo and crystal children. Because they have a higher vibration than the rest of us, this stone helps them to accept and adjust to their human form.

OKENITE

The okenite crystal helps you to understand how your past is influencing your present, so that obstacles are cleared from your path. It links you to your Higher Self, enabling you consciously to manifest your purpose and helping you to fulfil it. In doing so it enables you to complete your karmic cycles. This, in turn, accelerates your spiritual growth.

PETALITE

Petalite helps to purify your aura, enabling you to become very calm and clear so that you can link into the highest levels of spiritual knowing. It then assists you to speak of what you see during your spiritual visions.

RHODOCHROSITE

Rhodochrosite enables the physical and spiritual realms to integrate by acting as a bridge between the upper and lower chakras. Its gracious pink light teaches the heart to accept and assimilate life's experiences and hurts without closing down. This enables you to bring the energy of your higher centres into your life. It is the best crystal for helping and supporting people who have suffered sexual abuse. In addition, when you use it in meditation it helps you to clarify your individual life mission.

ROSE QUARTZ**

The rose quartz heals the heart. It is the beautiful crystal of love and nurturing, qualities almost everyone needs in the current times. When you work with this crystal, sleep with it under your pillow or wear it near your heart: it will nourish love within you. When your heart is whole, you feel joyous and at peace. You can also love unconditionally without expectation or attachment.

SMOKY QUARTZ**

This powerful stone stimulates you to release the unwanted aspects of yourself, such as desire for physical gratification, pride and escapist tendencies. It purifies you, inspires you to change your life to something better and helps spiritual energy to flow through you.

SUGILITE

This crystal heals through bringing underlying causes of stuck energy to consciousness. It enables you to understand the emotional and mental patterns that cause physical imbalances in your body and helps you to clear them and regain your health. It assists you in using this healing power wisely to help yourself and others. Indigo and crystal children will benefit from the understanding that this crystal can give them.

TOURMALINE*
Tourmaline: green, black and any other colour, helps to ground the universal laws on Earth and transforms limited human concepts into an expanded awareness. It encourages you to align yourself with the higher forces and channel the light into your life and the world.

EXERCISE: *Transmuting Energy*
To transmute lower energies into the higher frequencies of the spiritual and etheric realms, place an amethyst crystal at each corner of your bed. At night, when you go to bed, ask your angels to change and purify your anger, fear and other negative energies while you sleep.

EXERCISE: *Relieving Stress*
To relieve stress, sit quietly with the palms of your hands open and facing upwards. Place a smoky quartz in each palm. Close your eyes, breathe slowly and deeply, and feel the energy and warmth of the smoky quartz entering your body through your palms. It is like having the warmth of the sun travelling through you. You may well feel yourself shudder as it begins its relaxing work.

EXERCISE: *Working with Crystal Energy While You Sleep*
To bring the energies of any of the crystals we discuss in this chapter into your life, you can grid them round your bed simply by placing one crystal at each corner of your bed at night. As you sleep you will be absorbing the energy. Ensure that you only use one type of crystal at any one time.

EXERCISE: *Drawing In Crystal Energy*

For this exercise you will need a notebook and pen.

1. Sit in a chair with your feet flat on the floor and your spine straight. Light a candle and place it so that the flame is level with your eye.
2. In the palm of each hand, hold a crystal. (They must be the same type: two citrine, or two rhodochrosite, for example.)
3. Focus your eyes softly on the candle flame. Breathe slowly, deeply and rhythmically.
4. Feel the energy of the crystals entering your palms and spreading throughout your body. Sit like this for as long as you like.
5. When you are ready to end the session, close your eyes, close your palms around the crystals and raise your hands to your face.
6. Bring your closed hands to your third eye. Place them, still closed, with the top phalanges of your thumbs against the third eye. Sit this way for a moment or two and feel your third eye and the crystals communicating, exchanging energies.
7. When ready, lower your hands slowly, open your palms, and lay the crystals in front of you. Do not allow yourself to be distracted by anything or anyone in the room.
8. Finally, open your eyes and immediately note anything that you saw or any messages you received when doing this exercise. Keep your notebook consistently and see how the clarity and volume of information increases the more you do the exercise.

CHAPTER 26

The Year 2012

2012 is a prophesied period of great change. The Aztec and Mayan calendars stopped at this time for their Wise Ones could not see beyond that date, which was considered a time of the unknown. According to the Hindus, that year marks the pause between the in-breath and out-breath of Brahma, when time stands still for a moment allowing extraordinary things to happen. As we draw closer, it is essential that we prepare ourselves to receive the new energy that will be available at this time.

Winter solstice is set for 11.11 a.m. on 21 December 2012. At 11.11 a.m. there will be a rare astrological configuration of the planets, including Uranus, Pluto and Neptune, that only happens every 26,000 years and marks the beginning of a twenty-year transition for the Earth and its people, as well as starting a new 26,000-year cycle. In the past, because of the low consciousness of humanity, this alignment has coincided with events such as wars and changes in climate. This rare configuration will have a profound effect on us all because it involves the interplay of planets that have to do with the transformation of beliefs and attitudes, as well as qualities such as inspiration, creativity, imagination, spirituality, dreams and illusion.

Additionally, on this occasion, we have been given an eight-year period to prepare ourselves for the higher possibilities. One of the cosmic gifts we are offered is a special and auspicious line up, for it is very rare for Venus to transit the sun and when it does so it happens twice, with an eight-year period in between. The last pair happened in 1874 and 1882. In preparation for December 2012 a Venus transit occurred on 8 June 2004 and will be followed by the second one on 6 June 2012. This wonderful and special conjunction starts to balance the masculine-feminine polarity and offers everyone huge opportunities for growth and to accelerate their ascension and that of the planet. According to the Mayans, this transit represents a monumental rebirth of solar consciousness. It is important during the period between the two dates that we each do our best to help unite the world so that we can transform ourselves and the planet through spiritual awareness. This would involve creating a new consciousness that has respect for all forms of life and the planet's resources.

There are rumours of dire events in 2012 and counter rumours of enormous positive spiritual change on the planet. Which is true? Kumeka tells us that, right now, either outcome could prevail. He explains that the situation on Earth is like a seesaw that is currently balanced with positive and negative at opposite ends. We are asked to keep adding more and more focus to the positive end so that the planet will swing to the side of light, love and harmony. Each of us can and must do something about this while we have the opportunity. Every individual needs to make an active commitment to raising his or her vibration, which in turn will lift the frequency of the planet. This will contribute towards a positive outcome in 2012, and inevitably we will each receive huge benefits as we move closer to the golden energy that existed in pure Atlantean times.

The 2012 Winter Solstice also marks a time where a few people who are truly ready will transform and ascend. Others who could do so will instead stay to hold the light steady. It is also a time where some people will move on to the higher fourth dimension.

Kumeka offers the following message to humanity:
The 2012 Winter Solstice is a time at which something old will die and something new will be born. Throughout this book you have been given information that will allow you to develop a deeper spiritual consciousness, which is now much needed. In addition to this it is also important that you respect the planet on which you live and treat it with gentleness and compassion. In the name of ignorance many people are still destroying her beauty and vitality, so make it your aim to help people to move into a place of awareness regarding her needs. From the inner planes we will be doing what we can to aid you in raising your consciousness, but you, and the people you know, need to help your planet. What is the point of new consciousness if you have no planet on which to live and experience it? It is time for all of humanity to awaken to a true partnership with each other, the Earth and the cosmos, and by so doing become galactic citizens who care for and sustain the Earth, thereby sustaining yourselves.

There are four crystals that have been sent to help us prepare for this energy surge. By keeping these crystals with you, and meditating with them regularly, you will be able to raise your frequency and open yourself up to higher forces. (See the exercise 2012 Energy Building at the end of this chapter.)

SELENITE
As discussed in Chapter 16, this crystal has a very important role to play in the activation of the soul star. However, we can start accessing its energy right now. Selenite can show us how to bring the divine laws and principles into our lives. It can also teach us to combine spirit and matter so that we will be able to integrate the light force that is spirit into our physical bodies. In effect, spirit will find a home within each of us. This is a slow and gentle

process as our bodies and minds would not be able to adapt quickly to this new energy.

KYANITE

The main function of this crystal is to reconnect our energy with the causal chakra. Until we are ready for this, kyanite transmits a very gentle force to us that we are completely unaware of. Its energy is like a hand being held out to save us. We may be too afraid to see it clearly. Yet it is there and we only have to be ready to see it and reach out to make the connection.

It is believed that kyanite is more attuned to the etheric realms than it is to the physical realm. The higher powers of our minds have lain dormant for thousands of years and, as kyanite starts to rejuvenate these powers, we will access the ability to transport our physical bodies wherever we wish to go – without travelling by Easyjet. And that is only one of the many skills that we will reawaken. The changes necessary to our synaptic pathways would be too intense for this to happen overnight, but commitment to working with these crystals will build the pathways required.

Although kyanite may be relatively new to us today, it has been around for a very long time. When new souls were being born, the Atlanteans used it to address imbalances in the brains of those newly incarnated souls. Blue kyanite was one of the crystals used with selenite, hematite and calcite to open and clear the subtle energy pathways of the body. They also focused it on the meridian points to stimulate the flow of energy in the body and to clear energy blockages in the chakra centres.

These days kyanite can help the indigo and crystal children who are incarnating on Earth. When used by a qualified crystal healer, this crystal can assist in the treatment of epilepsy, autism, stroke symptoms and other forms of brain or mind imbalances. It does this by creating new lines of energy to connect the light source to the mind of sufferers.

CALCITE

Calcite's lesson is simple yet profound. It is here to teach us the art of 'being'. Working with calcite excludes the use of the mind as it simply wants you to be open to its teachings. It can bring you 'knowing' in its purest sense. Let us explain. How often has someone asked you a question that you have answered without thinking, but afterwards you realised that there was no way you could have known the answer. That is true 'knowing' and it comes from simply 'being'. When you work with this crystal it can alter the way you perceive reality. Like the kyanite, its energy is gentle so you will not experience an overnight transformation.

Working with calcite offers us many benefits. It is through this crystal that we will eventually be able to access cosmic knowledge that at this moment is beyond our understanding. It also helps you to know and understand the soul lessons that you have in-carnated to learn. Where you cannot comprehend the patterns or cycles that keep repeating themselves in your life, calcite will help you to achieve the necessary insight. It will also open up for you an intrinsic understanding of ways to resolve the situations.

HEMATITE

In the paragraph on selenite we explained that its purpose is to bring spirit into our physical body and to merge spirit and matter. Hematite's role is to connect the spirit into our blood stream. This allows the messages from spirit to become part of the genetic coding of each cell, thus establishing a blueprint of a purer and more vitalised energy within each individual. The amazing news is that new positive patterns will replace the old ones.

At this moment, Hematite is the main crystal on the planet that can activate the Earth Star and as such is the grounding element of this powerful quartet of crystals.

Kumeka wants us to know that although we talk about this new energy emerging in 2012, it is actually here NOW! When we access and use it, we will strengthen it.

Listed below are the crystals that are working with the chakras today to help us return to the pure energy of Atlantis.

Base chakra. Bloodstone, garnet, obsidian, blue onyx, smoky quartz, realgar, rhodonite and black tourmaline. These crystals enable you to work lovingly on the material plane and ground the spiritual forces into the physical body.

Sacral chakra. Amber, red or orange carnelian, citrine, ruby and wulfenite. These crystals help you to direct yourself towards your purpose and enable your creative forces to be fully utilised.

Solar plexus chakra. Apatite, calcite, citrine, sulphar and yellow or orange topaz. These will assist you with the digestion and assimilation of your experiences. They will also enable you to manifest your goals and use your personal power positively.

Heart chakra. Aventurine, dioptase, emerald, kunzite, malachite, morganite, peridot, rose quartz, rhodochrosite and green or pink tourmaline. It is time to release all traumas that we have suppressed emotionally, for these block the expression of this centre. The consciousness within these stones will help you to offer unconditional love through your daily actions.

Throat chakra. Blue lace agate, amazonite, aquamarine, celestite, chrysocolla, gem silica and turquoise. These crystals are dedicated to helping you to verbalise truth.

Third eye chakra. Amethyst, azurite, fluorite, lapis lazuli, sapphire, sodalite and sugilite. These will balance your state of mind and cleanse your third eye so that you can move into true devotion and perceive the Divine in all things.

Crown chakra. Diamond, heliodor, selenite, clear quartz and golden topaz. These help to bring you peace and wisdom in order to attain oneness with God. They will enable you to recognise your own connection with the Infinite.

EXERCISE: *2012 Energy Building*

Obtain one of each of the four crystals: selenite, kyanite, calcite and hematite. Please note that all of these crystals are very fragile and can be damaged by water, the sun and rough handling. The best way to cleanse them is by chiming Tibetan cymbals together and moving the sound round the crystals so that it penetrates and cleanses them. You can also use a singing bowl.

Keep the crystals with you at all times, putting them at the side of your bed each evening. They should always be within three feet (about a metre) of you, so you might like to wear them in a bag around your neck. As often as possible, preferably daily but at least once a week, carry out the following meditation using the crystals:

1. Ensure that you are in a place where you will not be disturbed. Light a candle and, if you wish, put on gentle, relaxing music. Close your eyes and get yourself into a quiet place where you are relaxed and centred.
2. Hold the crystals in your hands, with your hands together in the prayer position.
3. Bring your hands up to your heart centre and feel the gentle energy of the crystals connecting with your heart. See or sense a circle of energy that circulates from the crystals to your heart and back to the crystals again. As you are doing this, the crystals are attuning your body to their vibration. If the crystals were to use the full force of their energy, it would have too great an impact on you. Therefore the consciousness within them will automatically regulate their output to that which you are able to deal with. Please do not be concerned that they will overload you – they won't.
4. Sit with your hands like this for eleven minutes. (Eleven is a master number that possesses much more potential than other numbers. See Chapter 22 for more information about numerology.)

5. When the eleven minutes have passed, bring your hands up to your nose and mouth. Breathe the energy of the crystals in through your nose and mouth, then move your hands away and breathe out negativity. Do this three times. (This is a means of replacing the negativity that we carry with the positive energy from the crystals.)

Do not expect immediate results, since the effect of this exercise will be gentle. Indeed, it may take some time before you notice changes in yourself. However, it is important that we start this practice now because each time we do it we are helping light to accumulate at the positive end of the seesaw.

EXERCISE: *Crystal Meditation*
Choose a special crystal that you will programme for this use only.

1. Cleanse it in the flame of a candle or by wafting incense round it.
2. Sit with your spine straight. Imagine a golden cord going from your crown up in to the heavens. Feel the cord tighten and your spine straighten.
3. Take three deep breaths: in through the nose and out through the mouth.
4. Place both hands around the crystal, without touching it, until you can feel your energy field merge with the crystal's. Stroke the air around the crystal and the sense the air on your hands growing warmer.
5. Now stare into the crystal and chant *Ohm* three times.
6. Keep staring into the crystal until you feel as though you and it are one and the same.
7. Now see yourself stepping into the crystal. Once inside, let yourself become acquainted with its many aspects. Then move within it and be guided to see, hear, feel and/or be given what you need.

8. When you are ready to leave, see yourself step back out of the crystal.
9. Thank the crystal and open your eyes.

Remember to cleanse your crystal before and after your journey.

CHAPTER 27

Crystal Remedies and Essences

The powerful vibrations of crystals can easily be transferred to water. The crystal energy within the water then makes an essence which can be taken internally, applied to the skin or added to bath water. In some cases you can pour the mixture into a mister and use it as a room spray. Remember that water responds to your thoughts and intentions, so keep them pure and focused as you work with the essences.

Making a Crystal Essence

These essences are easy to make and can be taken either when it is not possible to carry or wear the specific crystals or to increase the effects of the crystals. All of these crystals are available, though some may be expensive and a little difficult to obtain. Not all crystals are suitable for use as an essence, as some of them can be harmful, even poisonous. Please see the notes on the specific crystals below for guidance. If you are in doubt, either consult a crystal therapist or simply do not use that particular mixture.

There are two ways of making a crystal essence, one direct and the other indirect. If you have chosen a toxic stone or a crumbly stone that will dissolve in water use the indirect method.

DIRECT METHOD

First choose your crystal and cleanse it, if required. You must use a non-crumbly, non-toxic crystal. Please note that all those listed, unless we clearly indicate beside them INDIRECT METHOD, come into this category.

Place the crystal into a glass bowl or jug with a pint of spring water and stand it in direct bright sunlight. (The best time to do this is between 8 a.m. and 11 a.m., when the day is fresh and new. However, this is not essential.) After three hours, remove the crystal and bottle the essence in a coloured glass bottle with an airtight stopper. To keep your crystal essence for more than one week, add 25% vodka or brandy as a preservative. Store in a cool dark place and it will keep for a year.

INDIRECT METHOD (FOR USE WITH CRUMBLY OR TOXIC CRYSTALS)

Those crystals that are toxic, crumbly, dissolve in water, or are very delicate and break or scratch very easily are clearly marked INDIRECT METHOD, and should be dealt with as follows:

First choose your crystal and cleanse it. Then fill a bowl with a pint of spring water. Place the crystal into a small glass jar and put this jar into the bowl, ensuring that no water gets into the jar. Stand it in direct bright sunlight for three hours.

After this time has passed, remove the jar and bottle the essence in a dark-coloured glass bottle with an airtight stopper. As with the direct method, to keep your crystal essence for more than one week you must put a preservative with it. Make a mixture of essence and 25% vodka or brandy. Store in a cool dark place and it will keep for a year.

This forms your stock essence, or mother essence as it is also known. This stock essence is used to make a dosage bottle by taking 10 to 20 drops of the stock essence and adding it to 2 ounces of a water-and-brandy mixture. This would then be the essence that you would use for treatment. Label your essences with the gem or gems used, the date made and whether it is a stock remedy/essence or a dosage bottle.

How to Use the Remedy

Either place 2 to 5 drops of the essence under the tongue 2 to 4 times a day, or place 10 to 20 drops in a glass of water and sip it throughout the day. They can also be used topically on the skin or put in bath water. You can add them to sprays to use for room or aura clearing. Be very careful when using lotions on your face, or when spraying in a room as they may get in your eyes and cause irritation. Alternatively, do not add alcohol to the essence when intending to use it near the eyes.

OILS

Non-crumbly crystals can also be placed in oils and ointments to use for skin care and massage. Taking the same crystals that you have used to make your remedy/essence, simply place the crystal in a high-quality oil or lotion suitable for your purpose, such jojoba oil for softening the skin, hazelnut oil for tightening and toning the skin, apricot or peach kernel oil for face treatments and macadamia oil for protecting against the ageing effects of the sun. Do not use nut oils on people with nut allergies.

Leave the crystal in the oil for 48 hours before using it and keep it there until you have used all of the oil. When the oil is finished, remove the crystal, wash it and re-energise it in the sunshine according to the original instructions.

Here are some of the crystal remedies used in Atlantis and their healing properties.

Agate. This stimulates the digestive process and relieves gastritis.

Blue lace agate. This was used during Atlantean times to treat brain-fluid imbalances and hydrocephalus, but today it is best known for its calming properties.

Moss agate. Apply this crystal remedy to the skin to treat fungal and skin infections.

Amazonite. This can help to address calcium deficiencies.

Amber. This can be used as an excellent natural antibiotic.

Aquamarine. An aquamarine crystal remedy works as a general tonic and has a strengthening effect. It harmonises the pituitary and thyroid glands, so it is helpful for sore throats, swollen glands and thyroid problems. It also assists eye problems, jaws, teeth and the stomach.

Aragonite. This relaxes the muscles, so it stops night twitches and muscular spasm. It also helps to heal bones.

Aventurine. Aventurine helps all kinds of skin problems.

Azurite. This crystal remedy, which was used a great deal in Atlantis, helps during a healing crisis.

Beryl. This was used to treat throat infections.

Calcite. Calcite is helpful when applied to skin ulcers, warts and suppurating wounds.

Cerussite. This was used as a spray to eliminate pests from house plants.

Charoite. This stabilises emotions during turmoil or crisis and is an excellent cleanser for the physical body.

Chrysanthemum Stone (INDIRECT METHOD)
This is helpful for dissolving growths and eliminating toxins.

Chrysoprase. The gentle chrysoprase calms stress, especially stomach problems due to anxiety.

Citrine. Crystal remedy made from citrine can help menstrual and menopausal problems.

Dioptase. This helps to dissolve headaches and pain.

Fluorite. This fights against viruses.

Galena (INDIRECT METHOD)
In the case of boils or inflammation under the skin, a cream was applied to unbroken skin to reduce inflammation and eruptions.

Hematite. (INDIRECT METHOD)
This helps to reduce fevers.

Herkimer diamond. The crystal remedy creates an excellent environmental spray. It also helps to reduce the effects of geopathic stress and electromagnetic pollution.

Howlite. Drops of this, taken regularly, balance the calcium levels in the body, which helps insomnia.

Jasper. This crystal remedy helps to balance the mineral content of the body.

Kunzite. This is a powerful crystal remedy, which is beneficial for psychiatric disorders and depression, and helps the body to recover from emotional stress.

Lepidolite. This crystal remedy helps with menopausal symptoms.

Moonstone. The remedy from this stone, which carries lunar energy, helps to relieve insomnia.

Snowflake obsidian. Used as a cream, this helps the skin, and as a crystal remedy is beneficial for the eyes.

Okenite. This soothing crystal remedy treats skin eruptions.

Opal. This helps to soothe the eyes.

Pyrolusite (INDIRECT METHOD)
By balancing the throat centre, this crystal remedy regulates the metabolism, strengthens the eyesight and treats bronchitis.

Rose quartz. This gentle crystal remedy soothes burns, blistering and any skin problem. Used as a cream, it smoothes the complexion.

Rhodochrosite. This crystal remedy balances the thyroid, soothes infections and aids the skin.

Rhodonite. This was used for shock or trauma in the same way that we use Rescue Remedy now.

Rhyolite. This crystal remedy gives people energy and strength and helps improve muscle tone.

Shattuckite. This makes a general tonic, particularly in the spring.

Sulphar (INDIRECT METHOD)
For external use only. A cream made from this crystal alleviates painful swellings and joint problems.

Topaz. This helps to sharpen the vision.

Turquoise. This strengthens the immune system, both physical and subtle, as well as the meridians and energy fields. It works as an anti-inflammatory and so it relieves cramps, gout and rheumatism. A crystal remedy from this beautiful stone can help to heal and detoxify the whole body, particularly the eyes (including cataracts).

Ulexite (INDIRECT METHOD)
The cream from ulexite helps to smooth wrinkles.

Unakite. This remedy aids the growth of skin tissue and hair.

Vanadinite. (INDIRECT METHOD)
A vanadinite cream, rubbed externally over the chest, aids breathing difficulties and congestion of the lungs. For those who often feel spaced-out or ungrounded, take the crystal remedy internally as a remedy for several weeks.

Zeolite. The crystal remedy can be taken to dispel bloating and to release toxins from the physical body. It can also be supportive in overcoming alcoholism.

Of course, in modern times, you should not use essences, remedies or creams in lieu of medical advice. Please see a doctor if you have a persistent problem. These days many people are incarnating with much personal, family and ancestral karma. This may mean that physical, mental or emotional conditions are deep-seated and may need medical intervention. In the earliest days of pure Atlantis, people incarnated free of karma so essences, remedies and creams were only needed to support or to help to rebalance.

CHAPTER 28

Master Crystals

As the chapter heading suggests, the crystals described in this chapter are the masters. Each one has its own specific purpose, but all exist to teach us about divine law and bring messges from the heavens. They have been programmed by Source for this purpose. We are blessed to have these crystals available in our crystal shops today, for it indicates that humanity is ready to receive and comprehend vast knowledge, ideas and concepts.

To work with these crystals effectively you will need to train your mind to be still. Use them with absolute respect and purity of intention. Because you do not want to have any other influences on your crystals, do not allow anyone else to touch them when you are actively working with them.

Channelling Crystals

In Atlantean times, everyone used a channelling crystal as a tool for personal meditation to access clarity and wisdom about their daily affairs. Also, when they wanted to ask questions or needed specific information about a situation, they would work with their own specially-dedicated crystals. They might use them, for instance, if they wanted clarity about the work they were to perform or guidance about a person they were thinking of marrying. It is exactly the same now. Most of us would like to be certain that our job, or the person we propose to marry, is right for us. In current times, the role of these crystals is to teach us how to tap into our own inner wisdom and bring forward our true, pure light from the depths of our inner being.

Channelling crystals that have been programmed by the ancient Alta of Atlantis are in existence. Those who are ready to receive these crystals will be attracted to them, and will instinctively know what work they are to do with them.

HOW TO RECOGNISE A CHANNELLING CRYSTAL

There would be a large, seven-sided face in the centre of such a crystal, with a perfect triangle on the reverse side. The number seven signifies the seeker, who is receiving information through the crystal; the number three symbolises his ability to express this higher knowledge verbally to the outer world.

EXERCISE: *Working with a Channelling Crystal*

Remember that absolute respect and purity of intention is important when using your crystal. When you work with a channelling crystal it is important that it is not subjected to unnecessary external influences, so please do not let anyone else handle or use it.

1. Close your eyes and focus on your breathing to take yourself into a deeply meditative state.
2. Hold the seven-sided face of the crystal to the brow chakra, the third eye centre, and take a deep breath.
3. Sit quietly and allow your mind to become still, open and receptive.
4. If you have a specific question, ask it, mentally.
5. Accept any images, impressions, symbols or feelings that come to you. Initially, the information may be vague or subtle, but as you practise with the crystal the information will flow more easily and effortlessly.

6. When you have finished, thank your crystal for the information it has given you.
7. Wrap it in a dark piece of natural material, silk if possible, and keep it in a safe place.

Laser Wands

In both Lemuria and Atlantis these dynamic and powerful crystals were used in the healing temples. They were also used to create energy force fields or protective shields around people or places, and were amongst those that helped to form the biodome over Atlantis.

In later days, when it became necessary for the rulers of Atlantis to discover, covertly, what was happening in the cities, they would use a laser wand to render themselves invisible so that they could move about undetected. They would not actually vanish, but a light would be projected around them that another person could not see through.

At the end of the final experiment of Atlantis, these laser crystals were withdrawn and stored in deep underground chambers to remain dormant until it was time for them to contribute their significant power to the healing of the people and the planet once again. By working with these crystals in personal meditation, it is believed that they can teach us the advanced-healing arts practised in Lemuria and Atlantis.

Not only do laser wands carry within them the knowledge of the Lemurian and Atlantean civilisations, but also that of the stellar spaces from which they originate. They serve to create a bridge between the earth and skies, the inner and outer. It is within these crystals that the secrets of laser-ray projection are stored. Currently we are only able to use a fraction of their potential.

In the right hands they are powerful healing tools, but in the wrong hands they could create much damage and negativity.

When we raise our collective frequency we shall be able to work with them fully once more.

HOW TO RECOGNISE A LASER WAND

These crystals are rarely beautiful on first viewing. They're more likely to be unappealing, but there is a purpose behind their form. It ensured that their power and real beauty can only be recognised by those who have learned the truth of outward appearance and have developed their third-eye vision.

Laser wands are long and slender, rather like fingers. Their very shape suggests that they can project and direct energy through them. A laser wand's power and knowledge increases the more it is used. Often these crystals carry markings that resemble hieroglyphics. The number of symbols indicates the level of power and knowledge held by that particular wand.

A unique aspect of laser wands is that their angles are not straight, but curved. However, they still hold a direct, uninterrupted frequency of energy, whether or not they are acting as transmitters at that time. Their form appears imperfect and yet in their energy, essence and projection, they are pure. This symbolises one of the main lessons that this crystal teaches.

WORKING WITH A LASER WAND

In the hands of very skilled and experienced people, laser wands can be used for psychic surgery, but this is a highly specialised skill and any operation must be performed by a qualified person as part of an ongoing treatment schedule, including counselling.

When using a laser wand, always hold the termination point away from your subject, when you are not purposefully directing it, because the energy beam could cut through a person's auric field. This is rather like cutting a hole in someone's overcoat, which could render him vulnerable to the cold and wind. In the case of making a hole in someone's aura, it could leave him open to negative thoughts or viruses.

EXERCISE: *Protect Your Home and Car*

Hold the wand between your hands, with the termination point at the tip of your fingers. Close your eyes and breathe deeply until you are relaxed. Bring your index fingers, still holding the wand between them, up to your brow chakra. Project the thought of your home or car being safe into the wand.

Once you have done this, open your eyes and stand with your back to your home or car. Raise your arm to shoulder level so that the termination point of the wand is pointing directly in front of you. Keeping the wand flat, point it away from you and your subject so that you are between it and the wand. Now feel the energy pulsing through the wand and walk all the way around the outside of your home or car with the wand pointing outwards. In your mind's eye see an impenetrable shield building around you and whatever you are protecting.

Thank the wand for its work and feel its beam return to a resting state.

EXERCISE: *Protect a Person*

Hold the wand between your hands, with the termination point at the tip of your fingers. Close your eyes and breathe deeply until you are relaxed. Bring your index fingers, still holding the wand between them, up to your brow chakra. Project the thought of the person being safe into the wand.

When you have done this, open your eyes and stand with your back to the person you are surrounding. Raise your arm to shoulder level, which means that you will be standing in their auric field with the termination point of the wand pointing outwards. Feel the energy pulsing through the wand and walk all the way round the person with the wand pointing outwards. In your mind's eye see an impenetrable shield building around you and the person you are protecting. If the person is lying on a table ready for healing, walk around the table with your back to the table.

Thank the wand for its work and feel its beam return to a resting state.

Transmitter Crystals

The transmitter crystal was used in Atlantean times either to access universal wisdom about a specific individual or particular set of circumstances, or to tune into cosmic truth. It tended to be used as a training tool for the Novices, but was also used by the Adepts for seeking information. One of the lessons that the transmitter crystal teaches is to refine thought forms and communication. It teaches clarity. Additionally, the crystal will direct your thought forms out into the universe to seek answers, which is why clarity is so important. The Atlanteans would use these crystals for interworld communication.

To be able to use a transmitter crystal you must feel worthy of receiving the information it brings back from the universe, so a process of self-purification needs to be undertaken before you can effectively use one.

Like the channelling crystal, the transmitter crystal also exhibits the 7:3 ratio. There is a perfect triangle in the centre of the crystal linked to two seven-sided faces, one on each side of the triangle. The numbers here are significant. Three represents personal empowerment, and is balanced by the pair of sevens, indicating the God-self or superconsciousness. The seven sides represent the seven qualities of freedom, joy, knowledge, love, manifestation, peace and unity.

EXERCISE: *Working with a Transmitter Crystal*
When using a transmitter crystal you will need to prepare an altar or special place where it can be left undisturbed and in an upright

position for twenty-four hours. Leave it where it will receive as much natural light – sunlight and moonlight – as possible, but where no one else can touch it. Where the crystal does not have a flat base, you will need to prop it up against a piece of natural wood. The most ideal time to programme a transmitter crystal is either sunrise or sunset.

Before you programme your transmitter crystal, it is important that you are very clear about your question or request, or the guidance that you seek. It is worth writing down your question and meditating on it to ensure that it is truly what you wish to ask. The old adage seems appropriate here: 'Be careful what you ask for, because you may get it.' To give an example: A man decides that he would like to work with the youth of today to help to expand their minds, so this is what he asks the universe for. Now, he is a drug dealer selling mind-expanding drugs. Be very specific in your request.

Once you have clarified your request, hold the crystal in your left hand. Close your eyes and relax, sitting quietly and breathing deeply. Concentrate on the qualities that the seven sides represent: freedom, joy, knowledge, love, manifestation, peace and unity. Clearly define the question in your mind and then slowly raise the crystal and hold the triangle to your third eye. Now project the question into the crystal.

Next day, at the same time if possible, sit quietly, close your eyes and align with the seven qualities. Still your mind completely and become very open, willing and receptive. Again, hold the triangle to your third eye and receive the information it relays to you.

When you have finished working with your crystal, thank it for the information that it has given you and place it upright on the prepared altar. It is very important, when working with a channelling crystal in this way, that it is not subjected to un-necessary external influences.

Earthkeeper Crystals

Many myths, legends and religious tracts refer to the beings that came from the sky to Earth and formed the Atlantean, Lemurian and Mu colonies. It was they who created the earthkeeper crystals. Once these extraterrestrial settlers had arrived to populate earth, the crystals enabled them to stay attuned to the higher frequencies of their far-off homes. They are very powerful crystals and anyone who comes within their auric field cannot help but be affected by their power. In the year 2000, earthkeeper crystals were excavated in Namibia, in Africa. Also, one of them is situated in Kauai's Island Temple in the Hawaiian Islands.

In Atlantis, these crystals were used by the High Priests and Priestesses to materialise food, water and all other things required by the people in the initial days of setting up their communities. The people had no idea of the power of the Alta, nor where all these supplies came from. It was through the misuse of this crystal, for their own personal gain, that the eventual downfalls of the Atlantean, Lemurian and Mu civilisations came about.

When the final Atlantean experiment had ended some of the settlers chose to stay. Eventually, they interbred with people from all the different tribes of Earth. The resultant genetic mix created a giant step in evolution. In effect, a new age of human was born and a new cycle began that will take aeons to complete.

At the end of Atlantis, there was also a mass exodus from the planet, so the earthkeeper crystals were buried within the earth. They literally became the keepers of the earth, and were to watch over and record all earthly events.

Although they are currently inactive, the earthkeeper crystals will soon be activated by those who carry the ancient knowledge. Then they will transmit the knowledge of the Earth's evolution to the Intergalactic Council, so that consciousness can be developed on other worlds. In order to activate the earthkeepers, we need twenty-one people who are willing to let go of their egocentric sense of self and instead consciously merge into a greater whole. Then we will be able collectively to link our consciousness to this knowledge and energy otherwise un-reachable.

The purpose of the earthkeeper crystals is to teach us the secrets of living in a physical body, in a material world, without being bound to it. Once they are reactivated we will again have the information and ability to live as they did in pure Atlantis.

HOW TO RECOGNISE EARTHKEEPER CRYSTALS

The earthkeeper crystals are enormous quartz blocks. The first one was discovered in 1986 just before the Harmonic Convergence of 1987. Earthkeeper crystals range from 7,000 to 8,500 pounds in weight, measure between five to seven feet (one and a half to two metres) in length and are usually found thirty to sixty feet (nine to eighteen metres) below ground. A few have been excavated and placed indoors and are used in meditation ceremonies. Of course, it is always better to meditate outside, with them in situ.

HOW TO WORK WITH EARTHKEEPER CRYSTALS

These crystals induce positive action. When a group works with them in meditation, individuals will be able to expand their idea of 'self' to include all the other group members. The group has awesome power to make positive change once it is unified heart, mind and spirit. As individuals learn to unite in this way, the planet will undergo a remarkable elevation.

Elestial Crystals

Before the final experiment in Atlantis, these crystals were created and imbued with the four elemental energies: earth, water, air and fire. Indeed, they can sometimes reflect the smokiness of fire by changing their colour and becoming smoky in appearance. They were then used by the representatives of the Intergalactic Council who visited Earth to cleanse, heal and reawaken the planet ready for the experiments to be carried out. Consequently, they are able to communicate supreme knowledge and cosmic consciousness.

Once the experiment was in operation, these elestials were used to help bring balance and well-being to the people. Their association with the earth element assisted the people to ground themselves in their new, heavier environment. They can be a great comfort to anyone experiencing death, helping them to release any fears associated with leaving the physical body and once again returning to pure soul energy.

RECOGNISING AN ELESTIAL CRYSTAL

These crystals originated in the celestial realm and they have been sent to Earth to aid with the worldwide cleansing, healing and reawakening that is happening here at this time. They will invariably be found near water and often have bubbles within them representing the air element. Unlike any other quartz crystal, they have no broken or dull aspects, but have natural terminations all over the body of the crystal, which gives them a great radiance. The most distinctive thing about them is that they have geometric patterns and markings that appear to have been etched and layered on. However, these are natural formations.

EXERCISE: *Working with an Elestial Crystal*

Elestial Crystals are incredibly powerful and you cannot play with them. Before you use this crystal you must have been properly taught by someone qualified and experienced in working with them. Imagine giving someone a loaded gun and sending him out to play: that will give you an idea of the danger of handling one of these amazing crystals indiscriminately. A gun in the hands of someone who respects it, and has been properly taught, is highly effective.

Today, their main purpose is to assist us in opening to the

celestial realms. However, in order to do this we need to have worked through issues of personality and ego so that we are a pure channel for their energy.

When you work with them one of two things can happen. For the person who has carried out enough of the work necessary to purify himself, the elestial will open the crown chakra and link them with the cosmic energies. If you have not yet purified yourself sufficiently, the elestial will assist by showing you what aspect of your personality and ego you need to work on. You may feel that your beauty defines you, or that you are special and different in some way. For instance, if you are proud of your intellect and have built up a strong identification around this, the elestial will show you how this belief is a mere shadow of truth when seen in the expanded picture.

For the person who is not ready to face these truths about themselves, the outcome can be devastating. So often we believe that we have worked with and cleared issues, then something happens to show us that they still have an influence. It is only when we are ready to deal with these aspects of self at the deepest level that the elestial is likely to appear in our lives. Elestials resonate with the heart, the mind and the soul, and when one appears in your life greet it as a friend. It is an indication that you are ready to assume your rightful angelic characteristics.

Window Crystals

In Atlantis, window crystals were used in a variety of ways. They assisted Novices and Adepts to reach deep inside themselves to understand what work they needed to do in order to find the purity that they were seeking. The crystal would reflect back to them the energies operating within them, then, with this knowledge, the Novice or Adept would be able to take the required action. Initiates would also use the crystals to read the auras of people, in order to determine their soul purpose. For instance, when a couple expressed the desire to marry, the window crystals were used to help determine the compatibility of the two people. They were also used to discover what role would best fulfil the soul purpose of an individual, and if a person or item was lost, the priest would project into the crystal a clear picture of whatever was missing, and watch for the feedback.

Atlanteans, who were prepared to go through the death experience so that their families could experience the related emotions, would use a window crystal as part of their preparations. Before they died, they were allowed to see beyond the physical world into the spiritual realms so that they could attune mentally to the soul level.

HOW TO RECOGNISE A WINDOW CRYSTAL
Window crystals are very rarely found, but if you are willing to look clearly and honestly at yourself you may attract one into your life. They have a diamond-shaped 'window' at the centre front of the crystal. This window is large and clear enough that you can see into the centre of the crystal. The tip of the diamond leads directly to the top termination and the bottom point leads directly to the base termination. The two side points connect with angles forming opposing faces.

The window crystals do not carry records or hold memories of what they have witnessed: they reflect. If you see something in one which makes you uncomfortable, recognise that it is a reflection of an aspect of you. It cannot be blamed on the last person who used the crystal.

These crystals are windows into the soul and allow you to see beyond any illusion, into the essence of the self. They are considered to be teachers and gurus, for they do not discriminate about what they show – be it dark or light – but simply reflect in picture form what they see.

Window crystals' power grows the more you use them. They

come to 'belong' to you and can easily assume the role of your meditation partner, encouraging you to go inside and view yourself.

EXERCISE: *Working with a Window Crystal*
Listed below are two methods for using a window crystal. Try both methods and choose which one you feel more comfortable with. It is purely a case of personal preference.

Method 1
1. Make sure you have a notebook and pen by your side.
2. Sit quietly, close your eyes and concentrate on your breathing until you are relaxed. Let your mind be still, empty and receptive.
3. When you are ready, open your eyes and look directly into the diamond window of the crystal. Do not stare but simply let your vision relax.
4. Accept whatever pictures it shows you. The more you use the crystal the easier it will be to perceive the pictures.
5. When you are ready, thank the crystal, lay it to one side and immediately make a note of the pictures. This is important, as the meaning of the pictures may not be immediately obvious.

Method 2
1. Make sure you have a notebook and pen by your side.
2. Sit quietly, close your eyes and concentrate on your breathing until you are relaxed. Let your mind be still, empty and receptive.
3. Reflect on the situation about which you want information.
4. When you are ready, place the window of the crystal against your brow chakra and mentally project into it an image of your situation. Then still your mind, relax and open yourself to receive the images the crystal will reflect back to you.

5. When you are happy that you have all the information, open your eyes and write the images in your notebook.

Whichever method you use, the meaning of the images may not always be obvious to you. If they are not, do not try to understand them immediately. Close your notebook, put it by your bed and leave it until the following day. During the night, or in the course of the next few days, you will find the meanings coming to you through dreams, from something you read, a casual remark made by someone, or by one of many other natural ways.

CHAPTER 29

The Fall of Atlantis

For 1,500 years the people of Golden Atlantis focused on co-operation, gratitude and honouring all life forms. As a result, during this entire time, they maintained inner peace, happiness and spiritual purity. This meant that only light angels, with incredible vibrations equivalent to our current archangels, entered the dome over Atlantis.

Because everyone drew from the Great Pool of Pure Energy created by the High Priests and Priestesses, they were able to keep the frequency high and develop amazing psychic gifts. The Magi especially were highly-trained, extraordinarily-skilled priests with powers beyond anything we can comprehend now. These powers they used in service to all. And then one day a Mage realised he could use the Great Pool for his own personal benefit. For the first time greed entered the consciousness of Atlantis and this allowed a dark angel to enter the continent. Soon the concept of personal gain and power spread and some of the Magi began to believe that they were better than other people. This state of ego created separation from the Divine and attracted in more dark forces. From that moment, over a period of 8,500 years, the experiment, which was the hope of the universes, devolved until it became too evil to sustain.

With the triggering of egos, fear and suspicion crept in. Of course, as soon as this happened the vibration went down and people could not sustain their psychic powers. What started at the top moved through the priesthood and into the populace, and many people began to lose their natural spiritual gifts.

Reiki

In the golden times of Atlantis almost everyone was a healer. The healer priests could channel very pure spiritual healing and they used it with the highest integrity. In those days, everyone was open and psychic and they prized these gifts highly. However, when greed, need and fear appeared in people's hearts and the social structure started to break down, many people lost their psychic abilities. These non-psychic beings were considered to be inferior and were cast out. Some were even used as slaves. In those devolved times, most of the priests and Initiates, some of the Magi and even certain High Priests and Priestesses had sold themselves to the power of darkness. The continent was cast into chaos and uncertainty. Those who retained the pure spiritual values prayed for help to stop this abuse and the Intergalactic Council invoked Source to send angels, who gave them symbols. These symbols were placed into the aura of those who were affected and attuned them to a higher vibration, which restored their psychic and spiritual gifts.

At the fall of Atlantis, the reiki symbols were taken to Tibet, where they continued to be used for healing and to attune people to a higher frequency. Some of the newly-attuned people started to use them for personal power until eventually it was decided that humankind could no longer be trusted with the energy of the symbols and they were withdrawn.

Thousands of years later some of them were returned to Dr Usui in Tibet, one of those who had so assiduously worked for the light in Atlantis, so that he could start initiating selected people into the use of the reiki again. For many years, they were kept a closely guarded secret passed on only by word of mouth. Now, however, more of the symbols have been returned through other channels. They are now widely used by a variety of healers to heal people and realign their frequencies to a higher level.

Separation from Nature

Feelings of separation meant that Atlanteans lost their sense of oneness with nature. Then they forgot to honour the living world. They could no longer comprehend the importance of observing the rituals and rhythms of seasons or planting at the appropriate phases of the moon. Nor did they love and nurture their plants as before, so the food produced was less abundant and contained considerably lower life force. Consequently, they needed more food to meet their needs and had to work harder to obtain it. They had less time for the leisure, contemplation and fun that had kept their energy so pure.

At that time even families felt separate from each other so they naturally cut off love and understanding from all creatures. They ceased to treat animals as equal but different. For some reason humans began to think they were superior, more evolved and with a right to control other species. They took the produce of their former friends without asking. They believed they owned their pets rather than having an equal relationship with them. For the first time since this experiment started animals began to fear humans and vice versa. Up to this time there had been no history of mistrust. Of course, these settlers had never been incarnated during the previous Atlantean times when dread between the species existed.

As time went on they started to cut down trees indiscriminately. The water became polluted because they no longer blessed it and filled it with higher energy. Instead of water flowing through their land with the energy of love, peace and wisdom, the liquid was tainted both physically and spiritually by the fear and anger of people and animals

As the centuries rolled by people became desensitised to pain.

They sacrificed animals and drank their blood, believing that it would give them animal courage and strength. They revelled in gory bullfights and set other animals against each other. The horses had always enjoyed racing for sheer pleasure, but now they were reined and ridden by humans who forced the creatures to perform. People gambled on the results. Towards the end of the experiment, cruel humans forced animals to work for them and trained them for war. They used them for fighting and to attack their enemies in unutterably cruel ways.

The high-frequency angels and unicorns withdrew from the planet. The great energies like the Silver Violet Flame, the Mahatma Energy and Reiki were taken from the people. Eventually, nature rebelled with earthquakes, volcanoes, poor crops, pestilence, hurricanes and floods. Instead of listening to the messages from Gaia, the Atlanteans fought nature and tried to control or change it. They genetically modified the seed for the crops, cloned animals and force fed them, and put the equivalent of silicone chips into humans and beasts.

Loss of Spirituality

As a consequence of the loss of their spiritual and psychic connections, discontent set in amongst the people. Without a higher vision for life, individuals became self-centred. They became greedy and ambitious, seeking material, sensual and sexual satisfaction instead of spiritual love. Life became a burden and they sought to forget the pain with alcohol, mood-altering substances, loud parties, orgies, heavy food and by being busy. Competition to show excellence became distorted into competition for personal prowess and self-aggrandisement. Discordant music became popular, reflecting the general mood.

When a couple married they began to exchange bracelets as a symbol that they belonged to each other. Before, they had been free spirits choosing to stay together with commitment and love.

Now, they felt chained and psychic cords started to strangle couples in relationships. During the Golden Age, right-brain activities, which maintained the spiritual and psychic connection, were practised. Creativity, artistic expression, social interaction, contemplation, meditation, music and playful fun were honoured. However, once the people and children could no longer draw in the teachings from the crystals or practise telepathy, the priests started to teach them to write as a form of communication. This developed the left brain. So now children were taught to read and write, study astronomy and mathematics. As they sought more and more knowledge, science and technology replaced spirituality. It became the God. The social aspect of storytelling deteriorated for they no longer had to maintain their right-brain powers of memory retention. Families and communities started to break up. Worry and busyness took over. People started to trade for money, which they then hoarded. Later, interest was charged on loans so the rich became richer and more separate.

At the height of Atlantis, everyone radiated the light of happiness and spiritual fulfilment. They needed no adornment to complement this, just a simple crystal to attune to their Higher Selves. As their inner light dimmed, personal appearance became more important and they compensated with elaborate clothing and jewellery. Those who felt socially superior wore richer clothes to demonstrate their elevated status. At the same time buildings became complicated and often inlaid with gems.

The ordinary citizens were no longer open to the high-frequency light poured down on them from the Temple of Poseidon. The healing energy was now wasted on them, but nevertheless those High Priests, Priestesses, Magi and Initiates who remained pure continued to beam it down onto the population because they hoped they could turn the tide back towards spirituality.

Gradually, too many people became unbalanced for the good

priests to help them all. Then those who resorted to criminal activities were shackled and imprisoned. Everywhere, the chakras of the natural healers closed down and open-hearted people who could still offer healing were treated as suspicious and were outlawed. Illness, disease, viruses and mental imbalances became rife.

In the pure times, people loved to give thanks outside in nature or in simple round buildings. But now, people worshipped indoors in increasingly elaborate temples. Thanksgiving became supplication as they felt fearful of the future and felt their needs might no longer be met. Those who had lived for so long in trust and simple faith were beset by survival fears.

Then they killed animals and started to eat meat without the permission of the animal, which rapidly coarsened their vibrations and diminished further their psychic abilities.

DEGENERATION OF THE PRIESTHOOD

Priests, who had been wise counsellors, friends and equals, now took control. They felt they were superior and proclaimed they were chosen ones, the only ones who had a direct line to God. They took power over their flock by falsely claiming that they communicated with their ancestors and with demons. They demanded money or loyalty from the people by threatening them with the vengeance of the invisible beings. Superstition increased, resulting in the establishment of dogma, for when something had a positive result it was repeated until it became their truth.

To express their superiority, temples were more elaborately decorated and at the same time the priests wore richer robes. Some of them started to wear rings to symbolise their unique connection with God. They also wore headgear to suggest that they could reach up to the divine and were therefore more important than the masses. The more senior the priest, the higher the hat. They also tried to disempower women, claiming that they were inferior, and made them wear a headscarf to symbolise this.

And they ordered men to be circumcised, mutilating their symbol of power.

Some of the highly-trained black Magi also used their vast occult power to frighten and control the people. For example, they would manifest dark and terrifying images, telling people that they would be consumed by them unless they fell in line.

Morality was deteriorating rapidly. As they no longer had ability to connect to the wisdom of the universe, Atlantis divided into factions, many led by black Magi. Even some of the High Priests and Priestesses became tainted and, because their powers were so vast, waves of evil spread round the continent.

The leaders sacrificed animals before meetings and drank wine mixed with animal blood to enhance their power. These rulers were feared and hated by the populace who they tried to control. They forced many of the citizens to become slaves or soldiers by placing conditioning boxes on their backs and remotely controlling them. Today the equivalent would be a silicon chip through which control is maintained.

LOSS OF DIVINE CONNECTION

The energy dome that contained Atlantis was weakened, so determined ones could go beyond its natural defences. No longer content with power within their homeland, the Atlanteans sought to expand their territories. As is inevitable, with morality deteriorating at home, the army became inhumane and merciless. Prisoners were mutilated and women were raped as a form of male domination and loathing. Darkness prevailed.

Before the commanders attacked a country, the dark Magi used techniques of black magic to gain power over the people that they wanted to conquer. Using their extraordinary weapons technology, Atlantis became an acquisitive empire contravening every spiritual law.

During the golden years, our planet radiated light into the universe and was the focus of much help and attention from certain evolved star systems. We received technological and scientific information, healing methods, wisdom and much light. As Atlantis devolved and the people lost their spiritual and psychic powers, they could no longer communicate with the Wise Ones of the universe. The people of Earth thought the beings from other planets were aliens and resisted and feared their guidance and help. We became isolated within the universe and the Illumined Ones watched in deepest concern.

PREPARING FOR THE END

The Intergalactic Council gave the people of Atlantis warning after warning. They were given many opportunities to change their ways, but they chose to continue with their debauched and profligate lifestyles and their gross misuse of power. At last, the use of technology and black magic to control the masses surrounded the dark ones with such a heavy, discordant vibration that the forces of light could no longer connect with them at all. They decided that the experiment had once more failed and must be terminated.

Of course, a flood did not submerge the continent overnight. The final phase took several hundred years as places had to be prepared for the light ones of the twelve tribes to inhabit. The High Priest and Priestesses, whether pure or evil, had to be replaced by the original ones, who had the training and ability to lead the tribes into their new life. The twelve crystal skulls had to be created and kept updated with all the understandings and wisdom available. Wherever they were held, the pure priestesses who looked after them must be ready to carry them into the outside world. Decisions must be taken about the Great Crystal of Atlantis. Should it be dematerialised and returned to Source? Or left on Earth, where its power could not be abused? It was decided to let it remain on Earth, so when the Temple of Poseidon was submerged under the waves the Great Crystal fell to the sea bed and now lies in the centre of the Bermuda Triangle. It cannot, of course, be seen by people with third-dimensional consciousness. But when the Intergalactic Council need to activate it for planetary purposes, everything within the vicinity goes through a rapid interdimensional shift and becomes invisible to human eyes.

PRESERVING THE WISDOM

Many of those who caused the fall of Atlantis came from Sirius. They were those who had brought to Earth information about technology and science, and then abused it for their personal glorification. Dolphins also come from Sirius and they were endeavouring to curb the excesses of their fellows from the same planet. Inevitably, those humans who had karma to repay when Atlantis fell were tied to Earth until it was repaid. For many this would take hundreds of incarnations.

A decision was taken to allow some of those who had originated in Sirius, and who had abused power in Atlantis, to take dolphin bodies when the continent finally submerged. In this way they were tied to Earth, but could no longer abuse power as they might if they reincarnated in human form. They still repay karma by maintaining the vibration of the oceans and by using their enormous power and understandings to give healing or bring joy to people. These dolphins have brains like vast computers in which they hold all the knowledge about Atlantis, including the reason that it fell. They are now starting to return the great knowledge telepathically to certain people as appropriate. Different sorts of dolphins each hold one twelfth of the knowledge.

All the wisdom, as opposed to knowledge, of the most glorious time was held by the angels of Atlantis; glorious, illumined, pure-white angels of incredibly high frequency. Throughout the universe many beings of questionable credentials want this information for their own aggrandisement and power. The angels of Atlantis sought somewhere to hide the information where no one would think to look for it. Where better than among those who had caused the downfall of the continent? They decided that they would also take dolphin bodies. Because these angel dolphins have a much higher frequency than the others, they cannot be harmed at present. The whales, turtles, sharks and other sea creatures are all committed to protecting the angel dolphins, with the aim of taking some of the wisdom back to their home planets when the time is right. However, as the seas are being polluted, they all become more vulnerable.

The angels of Atlantis are now looking for people who are pure enough and prepared to commit themselves to take some of the wisdom from them and start to spread it on Earth. This will help to bring back the energy of pure Atlantis.

And so, finally, Atlantis was submerged under the ocean. However, the wisdom of the golden times was not lost. It was spread throughout the world as the twelve tribes interbred with local people everywhere. This extraordinary knowledge is still within us, encoded into our DNA. And the secrets of its great wisdom and light are now being returned to us, offering us a glorious opportunity for spiritual growth and evolution.

CHAPTER 30

The Twelve Tribes

At the fall of Atlantis, the original High Priests and Priestesses each led one of the tribes to its new location. Here, the refugees interbred with the local people and shared their knowledge and wisdom with them. This resulted in a huge advance in civilisation worldwide. Because of their blond hair, blue eyes and glowing energy, and also because they were so advanced in comparison with the ordinary humans, they were considered to be Gods. The ultimate purpose of this merging of mighty ones with the populace was to enable more people to carry the wisdom of Atlantis in their genes. Now that people everywhere are seeking spirituality again, and the frequency of the planet is rising, this inherent genetic information is being released to enable the energy of pure Atlantis to return.

The twelve tribes eventually developed into the following cultures.

The Egyptian Connection

Thoth. He took his tribe to South America where they became the Incas, famed for their gold work. They were the priests and architects who built Machu Picchu and established the great two-way interdimensional portal there.

Isis. She came from the planet Venus and took her tribe to South America where they became the Aztecs, renowned for their magnificent art and their knowledge of the stars. The famous Aztec calendar began with the birth of Venus and calculations are based on advanced astronomical knowledge.

Horus. This tribe became the Babylonians, merchants and tradesmen who taught people how to trade with integrity according to spiritual law. They were the craftspeople of the buildings and gardens and developed the Hanging Gardens of Babylon.

Ra. This tribe became the Egyptian culture, which seeded the Pharoahs and took with it much medical knowledge and information about all natural therapies. They took with them the Sphinx and the design of the pyramids.

Sett. This tribe became the Innuit, who were shamans. They were connected with the element of water and had a symbiotic relationship with animals. They took with them many of the ancient stories and traditions.

Imhotep. The mighty High Priest of Atlantis was ruler of the tribe that took its wisdom to the west to form the Native American culture. The Cherokees were Wise Ones who carried the secrets of Atlantis. They brought their knowledge of shamanism and soul retrieval to the peoples, as well as their special abilities to work with dreams using dream catchers.

One of the gifts that was entrusted to them at the end of Atlantis was that of honouring the land including all things living in it and on it. The Native Americans have been keepers of the ancient wisdom of the Earth ever since. The Wise Ones of the tribes are now reminding humanity that it is important to tread lightly on the ground, for Earth does not belong to us.

According to ancient Cherokee tradition, their ancestors came from the Pleiades to the five islands of Atlantis, where they settled.

Then, at the fall of Atlantis, the tribe sailed to the Americas taking their wisdom with them.

The Greek Connection

Hermes. This tribe went to Hawaii and became Kahunas, who remembered for us the most powerful form of prayer: the Huna prayer. They also brought the powerful dolphin link with them.

Zeus. This tribe went to Tibet. They brought with them the qualities of stillness, peace and harmlessness to all creatures and developed it into the Buddhist religion.

Aphrodite. She originated from Venus and led this tribe to South America. They became the Mayans, famed for their knowledge of astronomy and mathematics, which gave us the Mayan calendar and the placing and building of pyramids aligned to the stars.

Apollo. Western astrology as we know it today has come to us from Mesopotamia, but it originated in Atlantis. This tribe also gave us irrigation.

Poseidon. This tribe went to Greece. They carried with them the information about the navigation of the planet by using the stars, tides and winds. They were great scholars and the library of Carthage contained sailors' charts in which a continent was depicted where the Atlantic Ocean now lies. They helped the people to develop medicine and healing.

Hera. This tribe went to New Zealand and became the Maori, who were mystics and shamans. They taught the people sacred chants, singing and the art of storytelling, as well as unique farming knowledge.

The Purpose of Dream Catchers

In Atlantis, the priests used dream catchers in dream analysis since they had the ability to extract the bad dreams from the web. Using this ability they were able to help people without them having to undergo the trauma of remembering nightmares. When Imhotep and his tribe left Atlantis this was one of the traditions they took with them. To this day, dream catchers are a part of the Native American Indian tradition and more and more people are becoming aware of them and starting to use them. In present times the purpose of a dream catcher is to catch your dreams as they pass over. The good dreams find their way through the centre of the web (see diagram below) and the bad dreams become tangled in the webbing and fade in the light of day. Below we give you instructions on how to make your own dream catcher.

EXERCISE: *Make a Dream Catcher*

1. Wrap an 8 to 10 inch (20–25 cm) ring with the material of your choice. Keep the material tight and do not let it get twisted. (The Native American Indians tend to use suede lacing.)
2. Glue both ends of the material to the ring and hold it in place with a peg until it has dried. (See Stage 1.)

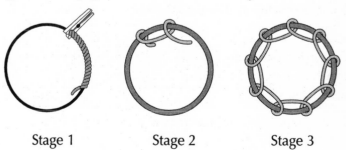

| Stage 1 | Stage 2 | Stage 3 |

3. Next, follow the instructions to create a dream catcher using natural or synthetic materials. Tie one end of the material to the ring and make loose half-inch (1 cm) knots around the ring, spacing them about 1.5 inches (4 cm) apart. Keep the twine taut between the knots. (See Stages 2 and 3.) When choosing what material to use for the web of your dream catcher, remember that it needs to be visible. Materials such as string or thick cotton or nylon can be used. A true Native American or Atlantean dream catcher would be made with sinew, for example catgut.

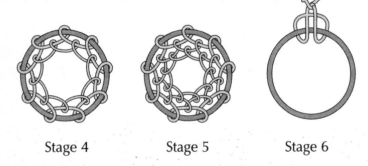

Stage 4   Stage 5   Stage 6

4. Make the next section of the web using the loops you have just created. (See Stage 4.)

5. Continue looping and knotting, keeping the twine tight. (See Stage 5.) Eventually you will have a small hole in the centre. Tie a double knot in the twine and put a drop of glue on the knot to make sure it holds. Once the glue has dried, cut off any twine that may be poking out.

6. To decorate the dream catcher you will need about 2 feet (60 cm) of string for attaching beads and/or feathers. Cut the string into 4 equal pieces and thread the beads or tie the feathers to the ends. Tie these decorative strings to the bottom, sides and centre of the dream catcher.

7. Be sure to attach a hanging loop to the top. (See Stage 6)

Huna Prayers

When we make a prayer and trust that it will be granted, it has already manifest. That is the Law of Prayer. However, most of us have doubts, fears and limiting beliefs stored in our unconscious minds, which block the efficacy of our prayers. Recognising this, a method of prayer was brought from Atlantis by the Kahunas of Hawaii which uses spiritual law to make supplications extremely effective.

They remembered that for many people the subconscious, conscious and the superconscious mind need to be involved for a prayer to be fulfilled. By using the power of all three aspects, the Huna Prayers are extraordinarily powerful. The Kahunas knew that our Higher Self, the original spark from Source, holds the perfect divine blueprint of who we are. This part of us knows we are divine and witnesses our personality on Earth. The subconscious mind, on the other hand, is where we store our beliefs, sense of worth, memories and repressed feelings. It is the Low Self, which lies between our conscious selves and the Divine, and it often blocks us from receiving the answer to a prayer. Then there is the conscious mind, the part that lives in the present and is aware. This part of us is able and willing to accept the bounty and consequences of our prayers.

The Huna prayer implements two factors that enable prayers to be successful. First, our conscious mind must raise enough energy to propel the prayer through the unconscious mind to our Higher Self. This is achieved by dance, invocation, chanting, clapping or anything that will increase our vital force. Second, once the prayer has actually been received, our Higher Self can then connect with the angelic forces and Illumined Ones who can help to bring our request about. They teach us to repeat the prayer three times and do this daily for thirty days. The repetition impresses our subconscious mind like an affirmation and helps to dissolve the blocks.

STEPS FOR THE HUNA PRAYER

1. You need to clear the path to your Higher Self by purifying yourself. When repeated before you say your Huna Prayer, these purification techniques really clear your aura. For example, you can write down and burn your anger, you can call in the Silver Violet Flame (see Chapter 14) or you can make the following forgiveness affirmation, either aloud or mentally, before the Huna Prayer:

> *Forgiveness Affirmation for Purification before the Huna Prayer*
> *I forgive everyone who has ever hurt or harmed me, consciously or unconsciously, in this lifetime or any other, in this universe, dimension, plane or level of existence or any other.*
> *I offer them grace.*
> *I ask forgiveness for everything I have ever done to hurt or harm another, consciously or unconsciously, in this lifetime or any other, in this universe, dimension, plane or level of existence or any other.*
> *I ask for grace.*
> *I forgive myself for everything I have ever done to hurt or harm another, consciously or unconsciously, in this lifetime or any other, in this universe, dimension, plane or level of existence or any other.*
> *I accept grace.*
> *I am free. All chains and restrictions fall from me. I stand in my full power as a master.*

2. Address your prayer to the being or beings of light you wish to respond to it. For example, you might like to start your Huna Prayer with: 'Beloved Buddha, Jesus, Mary, Allah, Mohammed, St Germain.' Or simply with: 'Beloved Source.' It is your choice whether you call on one or many.

3. Write down clearly and simply what you wish to manifest.
4. Raise your vital force by dance, chant, visualisation, clapping, decree, etc. A decree is a command to the universe.
5. Say your prayer aloud three times. End with a loud and clear, 'So be it. It is done.'
6. Direct your subconscious mind to take the prayer to your Higher Self with all the vital force, mana, chi, prana or energy necessary. Picture it shooting through your subconscious mind and out of your crown.
7. Relax for half a minute after this is done so that your lower self is not distracted. You might like to say *ohm* quietly.
8. Sit with your palms up, which is a receptive position, and say, 'Lord, let the rain of blessings fall.'

As with all prayer, you must be willing to listen for a response. You must be prepared to take action if you intuitively feel it is right. Include in your prayer something for which you are grateful. You can, of course, incorporate more than one request in your prayer.

EXAMPLE OF A HUNA PRAYER
Beloved Source, I now ask and pray with all my heart and soul for a relationship with a partner that will be mutually loving and fulfilling [this can be replaced by your individual desire]. I thank you for the opportunity to express love in my life [this can be replaced by anything for which you wish to express gratitude].

You should repeat the prayer three times. Then say, 'So be it. It is done.'

Now say, 'Beloved subconscious mind, I hereby ask you to take this prayer with all the energy needed to bring it to reality through my Higher Self to Source. Amen.'

Wait for 15 to 30 seconds as you visualise the prayer shooting up through your subconscious mind and crown.

Make sure that your palms are upwards and receptive, then say, 'Lord, let the rain of blessings fall.'

EXERCISE: *Create a Huna Prayer*
Using the example above create a Huna Prayer for yourself.

EXERCISE: *How Will You Be Remembered?*
Get a group of friends together and each tell a story about the legacy you are leaving behind for the next generations. We do not mean money. For example, is your legacy the people you have helped, the love you have shared, the children you have taught? Or is it, perhaps, the trees you have planted, the waste land you have cleared, the litter you have picked up, the animals you have cared for, the healing you have done, the people you have lifted with your smile or the wisdom you have shared?

CHAPTER 31

Preparing for the Energy

The times ahead are exciting and vitally important for you as an individual and for the planet as a whole. If you wish to be one of those who help to bring the energy of Atlantis back, you must be able to carry a high frequency light. Here are the steps that will help you to attain this at a cellular level.

Cleansing

Water has cosmic cleansing properties, so a shower or bath is much more than a wash: it psychically cleanses too. The more conscious you are that you are receiving a spiritual purification, the more effective it is. So when you shower, bathe, wash or swim, be aware that the energy of the water is penetrating into your cells and open yourself up consciously to inner cleansing. Even when you walk by water, bless it and call in its power of purification. As with all things, the purer the water you bathe in, the better. Remember to call in the Silver Violet Flame to transmute negative thoughts and words or anything that is not in harmony around you. Visualise it and sense it actively freeing you of psychic pollution.

Relaxing the Body

1. Stretch up, breathing in, then fall forward with an *aah* sound – focus on releasing tension. Repeat three times.

2. Shake out your shoulders and then the rest of your body.
3. Slowly make circles with your head in each direction.
4. Bend over and tap your spine with the back of your hand upwards, and as high as you can, while at the same time making an *uuuuh* sound. If you cannot do this then ask a friend to do it for you.
5. Tap the chest and make an *aah* sound in a Tarzan-like manner.
6. Massage the muscles between your ribs for a few moments.
7. Lie on the floor with your knees bent and feet flat on the floor. Gently ease yourself until your spine is flat. Relax and focus on your straight-yet-relaxed spine for as long as you like.

Healing

The physical, emotional, mental and spiritual bodies need to be healed as much as possible to allow through the high energy that is now bombarding our planet. Walking in nature, receiving hands-on or absent healing, and checking and balancing your physical body are all important. For the healing of the emotions and mind, it is necessary to watch your feelings and thoughts very carefully. You can cancel them in the Silver Violet Flame or write down the negativity and burn the piece of paper. Then remember to write down positive replacements.

Maintaining a High Vibration

The spiritual body is kept pure by wholesome reading, spending time in meditation and contemplation, attending higher-frequency talks or workshops and, of course, prayer and thanksgiving. Prayer, sacred chanting and beautiful thoughts keep your frequency high.

Letting Go

Again, we need to release physical, emotional, mental and spiritual attachments. You can do this symbolically by clearing out the clutter in your home. Of course, you must not replace it with more junk. Diana heard a lovely story that illustrates this. A friend of hers cleared out his garage, which took several journeys to the tip. For the first time he had room to put his car in the garage. But as he looked at his battered old jalopy, he realised that he did not want to put it into his clear, clean and tidy garage. He left it outside and told the universe he wanted to replace his car with something better. That was a very powerful, symbolic message and the following day he was given an unexpected pay rise, which enabled him to buy a new car.

When we detach from the need for possessions, people, beliefs and understandings on a regular basis, it keeps us free. Material goods are known as trappings because they trap our energy as we try to hold on to them. Of course, it is fine to have lovely things, but when we need them for our sense of worth they have power over us.

EXERCISE: *Setting Yourself Free*

1. Find a place where you can be quiet and undisturbed.
2. Light a candle and dedicate it to your freedom, for the highest good. You do this for the highest good in case you have a contract with someone or something to give them your energy for a period of time.
3. Close your eyes and breathe yourself into a relaxed and comfortable state.
4. Let a person, situation or object to which you are attached appear in front of you.
5. Tell this person, or even the situation or material possession, that you now wish to release it.

271

6. Imagine the cord that links you to him, her or it. The cord may be of steel. It may be strangling one of you. It may be thick, thin, coloured, malodorous or like a shifting cloud. It may reach out and entangle other people too. Let yourself feel it.

7. In whatever way seems appropriate to you, cut the cords and then make sure all their roots have been pulled out from both sides. You may like to ask Archangel Michael to help you with this.

8. Throw the roots onto a fire and watch them burn. If you wish to, you can burn the clothes you are wearing in your inner scene too. You may want to cleanse yourself in a stream or waterfall. Envision yourself doing whatever is needed to purify yourself and give a strong message to your unconscious mind that you are serious about the release.

9. Thank the person, object or situation for serving your growth.

10. Open your eyes and blow out the candle, thanking it for using its light to help to release you.

Strengthening

This is about increasing your levels of self-worth and confidence, in other words claiming your power.

One effective exercise that Shaaron often gives to people is to challenge them to do things that they have never done or experienced before. It may be as simple as taking another route to work, or going to the pictures alone, or riding on a bumper car at the fair, or inviting someone you would like to know better to a meal. These small things take you out of routine and strengthen you slowly. However, you can also expand the possibilities of your life. If you are afraid of driving in unknown places, once a week, drive into a new area and explore it. Have you long wanted to move house? Take the plunge. All the challenges around this will make you stronger. If you want to visit a particular place – do it.

Every person finds different things challenging. If you do a new thing every week, and something bigger once a month, you will soon be an infinitely stronger and more confident person.

EXERCISE: *Daily Exercise to Strengthen Your Muscles and Organs*

When our bodies are strong and toned, we carry more oxygen, are healthier and are physically able to hold higher frequencies.

A walk a day is wonderful for your physical well-being. We did not say stroll: take an energetic walk. Jogging, swimming, playing tennis, climbing, sailing, dancing or doing any exercise that uses almost all of the body will tone up your being. A visit to the gym three times a week would give overall exercise though an outside activity, if possible, is better. Start to make an exercise plan now.

EXERCISE: *Deep Breathing*

This exercise enables you to relax deeply at a cellular level so that your inner potential can be realised. It will increase oxygenation and expand your lungs.

1. Stand in a relaxed position, feet apart, and arms by your sides.
2. The following breath should be taken with your elbows coming up and out at your sides so that your lungs expand:
   * On a slow deep in breath, cup your hands in front of you with your elbows bent.
   * Bring your hands to your abdomen.
   * Take your hands to your armpits.
   * Stretch your arms to either side.
   * Reach up above your head, letting your hands meet.
3. Breathe out slowly as you bring your arms, outstretched at the side, down to the starting position.
4. Repeat as many times as you can.

EXERCISE: *Detox Your Body*

Toxins block our channel to the Divine. They clog our cells and slow our physical and mental processes.

1. Stand with your feet hip-width apart, your knees soft and your arms by your sides.
2. Raise your arms slowly, gathering energy, until they meet above your head.
3. With palms open and facing the ground, slowly bring your hands down in front of you to your abdomen. Visualise yourself pushing out stale energy.
4. Imagine your hands are collecting a ball of energy.
5. Turn your hands again to face the floor.
6. Bend slowly and place your hands over your knees.
7. Sense all the toxins flowing out through your feet.
8. Repeat several times.

Proper Nutrition

You are what you eat, or – to be more accurate – you are what you digest. Foods that you cannot assimilate clog up your system and slow your vibration. Not only that, but they make you feel sluggish and damp down your natural life force. Dairy products and fried foods come into this category, although psychically-sensitive people often have delicate digestive systems and cannot absorb a variety of foods. A basic principle is to eat as much locally-grown, fresh organic food as possible. Plants, vegetables and nuts have a pure vibration. Fish has a coarser frequency, while meat is grosser and also contains the fear of the animal during its life and as it was killed.

In pure Atlantis, when the people were natural vegetarians, all were blood group A. In later Atlantis, the groups mutated to allow meat to be digested. After Atlantis, as the experiments merged throughout the world, the groupings altered to include O, AB and

B. However, everyone must eat what feels intuitively right for them and some blood groups need meat. It is spiritually better to eat organically-produced meat with love, gratitude and reverence, than to be a vegetarian who is one because it makes them feel superior or who criticises carnivores.

Be very moderate about your intake of wheat, caffeine, colas, sugar and alcohol.

Enjoy and bless all your food!

Joyful Play Time

Kumeka says that play time is more important than most of us realise. Many of us are so focused on being busy, earning a living or even taking spirituality too seriously, that we forget to keep life simple. Laughter, joy, innocent fun and companionable pleasure are important to keep us light, healthy, happy and connected to the Divine.

Make a play list on which you record all the fun things that you love. Do you enjoy dressing up and playing charades? Don't groan. If you love acting games, write it down on your play list. If you love swimming, do you make it a serious business as you count the laps or do you let yourself have some fun too? Diana used to go lane swimming and she made herself swim for an hour, which she found pretty tedious. One day her son accompanied her and he managed to turn it into fun by swimming under her, coming up behind her and tickling her feet, making her laugh. Do what you love to do and lighten it up.

When did you last have a picnic or paddle in a stream or climb a tree? Life is not meant to be a heavy journey and when we travel together it can be joyous. Every time you do something on your play list, reward yourself with a big tick.

Blessings

Remember constantly to bless everyone and everything. No one need be aware you are doing it. Put your hand out and mentally bless the puddles as you pass and thank the rain that made them. Fill them with love, peace, joy and any other qualities you can think of. Bless strangers and friends alike. Bless cars that pass and their occupants. Bless and thank the trees and all of nature. It is often much easier to give than receive. Keep it in balance. Open yourself up to receive blessings from the angels, great masters and guides who surround you in the invisible planes. If you can visit a master who is incarnate in a physical body, take the time and trouble to travel there and receive the dharshan, divine blessing that comes through them. For example, Amma, the hugging mother, travels worldwide opening people's hearts and giving them wonderful blessings. Her website is: www.ammachi.com

We are living in the most important time of opportunity. Until now, there has never been a period in the history of the entire planet when our souls have had this chance of enlightenment and ascension. You are entrusted by spirit to bring back the energy and magic of the most spiritual time there has ever been: the Golden Age of Atlantis. When you decide to offer yourself to be a carrier of light, you will transform your life and that of your friends and family and everyone you touch. Your soul will receive rewards beyond anything you can currently envision, both in this life and during your onward progression. This is a time for celebration, thanksgiving and action. The tools you need are all within these pages. May the angels of Atlantis bless your journey.

List of Exercises

Here is a list of the exercises contained in this book, including the page numbers. Work with the ones that have 'spoken' to you as you read the book and embrace them as an essential part of your path towards ascension. Most of all, have fun with them!

Further Reading

Cooper, Diana, *A Little Light on the Spiritual Laws,* Hodder Mobius (2001)

Cooper, Diana, *New Light on Ascension*, Findhorn Press (2004)

Resources

Atlantis Oracle Cards by Diana Cooper, Findhorn Press (2005)
A pack of 44 beautifully illustrated oracle cards for inspiration and guidance. Each card carries information about Golden Atlantis that is relevant to you, personal guidance and a unique image. Available from retailers and www.dianacooper.com

The Diana Cooper School of Angels and Ascension teaches people how to facilitate workshops on angels and ascension. For full information about the School, its activities and courses visit: www.dianacooperschoolofangels.com

A Soul Reading by Shaaron Hutton can help you to understand and attain your purpose in this lifetime. For details go to www.shaaronhutton.co.uk or send for a leaflet to 73 Hornhatch, Chilworth, Guildford, Surrey GU4 8AZ.

Crystals can be obtained from: www.livingdesigns.co.uk

Bibliography

Andrews, Shirley, *Atlantis*, Llewellyn Publications (1997)

Decox, Hans, with Monte, Tom, *Numerology: Key to Your Inner Self*, The Berkley Publishing Group (1994)

Emoto, Masaru, *The Hidden Messages in Water*, Hado Publishing (2004)

Gilbert, Adrian, G., and Cotterell, Maurice M. *The Mayan Prophecies*, Element (1996)

Hall, Judy, *The Crystal Bible,* Godsfield Press (2003)

LaBerge, Stephen, PhD, and Rheingold, Howard, *Exploring the World of Lucid Dreaming*, Ballantine Books (1990)

Mails, Thomas E., *Secret Native American Pathways*, Council Oak Books (1988)

McMoneagle, Joseph, *Mind Trek: Exploring Consciousness, Time and Space Through Remote Viewing*, Hampton Roads Publishing (1993, 1997)

Melody, *Love is in the Earth: A Kaleidoscope of Crystals*, Earth-Love Publishing House (2004)

Newman, Hugh, *The Psychic Children*, Planet Art Publishing (2004) www.psychicchildren.co.uk

Raphaell, Katrina, *Crystal Enlightenment*, Aurora Press (1985)

Raphaell, Katrina, *Crystal Healing*, Aurora Press (1987)

Raphaell, Katrina, *Crystalline Transmission: A Synthesis of Light*, Aurora Press (1989)

Targ, Russell, *Limitless Mind: A Guide to Remote Viewing and Transformation of Consciousness*, New World Library (2004)

Tolle, Ekhart, *The Power of Now*, Hodder Mobius (2001)

Tulku, Tarthang, *Openness Mind*, Dharma Publishing (1978)

Yogananda, Paramahansa, *Autobiography of a Yogi*, Rider (1950)

HODDER
MOBIUS

**Transform your life
with Hodder Mobius**

For the latest information on the best in
Spirituality, Self-Help,
Health & Wellbeing and Parenting,

visit our website
www.hoddermobius.com